MW01518213

nick nolte

BY MEL WEISER

NOVELS

The Trespasser (Avon)
Within the Web (Dell)

PLAYS

Merci, Mercer! (A musical with Johnny Mercer)
Cry, Tiger!
Sweet Are the Roots

FILM

Love Ya Tomorrow (Arigam Pictures, Ltd.)

DIRECTED NICK NOLTE IN:

Middle of the Night
Five Finger Exercise
The Owl and the Pussycat
The Waltz of the Toreadors
Orpheous Descending
The Royal Hunt of the Sun
After the Fall
The Rainmaker
The Physicists
Requiem for a Nun
The Firebugs
      Among other stage productions…

nick nolte

caught in the act

by

mel weiser

Momentum Books, Ltd.

Momentum Books, Ltd.
Troy, Michigan

Copyright © 1999 Mel Weiser

Photo of Vicki Lewis by Johnathon Exley
Photo of Thandie Newton by Arnaud Borrel
All other photos by Mel Weiser

Printed in the United States of America
10 9 8 7 6 5 4 3 2 1

ISBN: 1-879094-59-2

Library of Congress
Cataloguing-in-Publication Data
Weiser, Mel.
Nick nolte: caught in the act/by Mel Weiser
p. cm.
ISBN 1-879094-59-2
1. Nolte, Nick 2. Motion picture actors and actresses—
United States—Biography.   I. Title.
PN2287.N565W45 1999
791.43'028'092—dc21
[B] 99-18046
CIP

To my two wonderful sons, Brenn and Darin,
whose interest in my work never flags,
whose assistance is always beneficial, and
whose love has been one of the great joys of my life.

Acknowledgments

What do I do when I complete a book? If I were unlucky, I'd send it directly to an agent or a publisher and hope I'm right about its condition. But I'm not unlucky. As a matter of fact, I'm extremely fortunate because I have some dear friends who are always there for me, astute readers who dive eagerly into the finished manuscript and give me the benefit of their intelligent insights and their sensitive reactions. They were there for me once more and, now, I want to thank them publicly for their years of friendship and for their selfless help with this book.

Alan and Charlene Jeffory
Elayne Stein
Sheila Paige-Roth
Mildred Fischer
Jay and Roxan Cohen
Richard and Sylvia Seader

I thank all of you again and again.

Portrait of the Artist at Work

Prologue

"Nick, I think it's time."

"For what?"

"A biography."

He looked at me with a grin. "You think so? Y'know, my agent wants me to do a biography for A&E."

"Don't do a television biography," I objected.

"Why not?"

"They're superficial. They just touch on events. Do a book. Show the inner man. Show how acting has shaped you. The whole process. What you've become."

"And you want to write it," he teased.

"Hey, I've been keeping a journal and making notes on you for years. You know that. Someday, I'm going to write about you one way or another, and you know that, too, don't you?"

"What would you write?"

"Something special. Something that shows the real you. Inside stuff. Not what's in all the interviews. That's all nonsense. Remember when you were moving your studio? You had all these boxes of your stuff that you were going to throw away? I told you to keep them. Did you?"

"I kept them."

"That could be a starting point."

He laughed. "We'll see. Lemme think about it."

The subject didn't come up again for months. When it did, it came up in the most interesting way.

"Are you and Vicki all right?" I had asked.

Vicki Lewis and he had met on the set of one of his films.

"We're going through something. We'll work it out."

"What's the problem?"

"She's getting to be a star, and it scares the shit out of her. She's confused."

"Why should that scare her?"

"Because she *knows*. She sees what it does! Fuck, man, this whole business of success and celebrity is a bitch! Success never supplies enough satisfaction! All it means is materialism, the acquisition of things! You find yourself in competition with everybody else in the industry, because if you don't have something and everybody else does, you feel you're nothing!"

"You don't have to—" I started to say. But he cut me off. He jumped to his feet. He became impassioned.

"You have to! I once told Streisand I felt rich and successful. Man, you should have seen her. She got fucking angry! She said, 'You're not rich!' And I said, 'Well, I've got a few million.' And she said, 'That's nothing!'"

"What would be rich to her?"

"Who the fuck knows? A *hundred* million!!!" He was shouting angrily, now.

"But to somebody like Bill Gates, she's not rich, either," I offered.

"That's *right!* Look at Rupert Murdoch. He can't get enough. His kids never saw him!"

"So, you're saying, Vicki is afraid of her success?"

"Exactly! Success creates fear! You get afraid that you never have enough, that in comparison to others you're nothing, and that you can lose whatever you have!"

"And what about celebrity?" I asked.

"Celebrity is poison! Everybody treats you unrealistically. They don't know shit about you, and they think you're special! That's bullshit! That's crazy! But pretty soon you begin to accept the bullshit and believe it yourself. You're in a position of authority and authority corrupts! It does! It *has* to! And soon you don't know who the fuck you are anymore!"

"Then you, Nick Nolte, you're trapped by success and celebrity, too, is that what you're saying?"

"You can't escape it! If you fight it, everybody in the industry thinks you're crazy; if you isolate yourself, they think you're crazy; and if you go with it, you *are* crazy! You're trapped! That's what's happening to Vicki now. She's becoming successful, and she doesn't know how to deal with it, so we're having troubles."

Vicki came in just then and asked, "What are you two talking about? I could hear the shouting all the way outside."

Nick answered as though he'd been caught talking about her behind her back but didn't want to appear apologetic. "Oh, we've been talking about success and celebrity. We started with you, but it's about all of us— you, me, everybody."

"What were you saying?" she asked.

"That it fucks us up. It takes us away from what we are."

The conversation went into metaphysical speculation about what we are, and how it's impossible to find that out in an industry that forces everyone to be something else, not only on screen, but in life. Nick became quieter, more earnest in voicing his views, as if he were trying to steer Vicki's thoughts away from the fact that he'd been caught talking about her.

Vicki just smiled. She understood. She's an extremely intelligent, fast-thinking woman.

I asked her, "Is he boring you?"

She nodded. "It's repetitious. It's all he ever talks about."

We laughed at that, and in the laughter I said, "Nicko, I wish I had a tape recorder going on all of this. It was great. That's the kind of stuff I'd include in a book on you."

He grinned shyly. Looking at Vicki with a phony, but engaging, touch of humility he asked, "Why would any-one be interested in me?"

She shrugged comically.

"It's not for others, Nick," I answered. "We do things like that to pull everything together for ourselves. We get a clearer picture of what we're all about. A book would be about you, of course, but it would be *for* you. It doesn't matter who would be interested in it. Hell, man, I have two novels sitting on my shelves that no one has ever seen. They were written for *me*. To clear some things up for me. Maybe someday I'll have them published, but that's not the reason they were written. Same thing for a book about you."

Smiling, he shook his head. "I don't know," he said. "We'll see."

Nothing more was said on the subject for a few days.

I was leaving Los Angeles, but I'd promised to visit with Sherri Wilson, Nick's wonderful secretary, before taking off. Knowing the gate code, I let myself in and went directly to her new office. Our greeting was warm and friendly, as it always is. But after a few minutes of pleasant chatting about her lovely surroundings and how happy she was to be working for Nick, the mood was shattered by his sudden appearance.

He stormed into the room. His face was dark with anger. He shot a cold, perfunctory greeting at me, and then directed the full power of his fury at Sherri on a matter so trivial, it was ludicrous. Something about an expenditure that amounted to a few dollars. This from a man whose indifference to money can have him spending thousands freely on things he may never use.

A gentle, pleasant woman, Sherri Wilson has faced her boss's rage numerous times. She knows exactly how to deal with the moment. She countered his accusations and warnings with a few simple explanations and then settled into a quiet acceptance of the madness until he'd exhausted his argument.

Finished with her, but still puffed with passion, he turned to leave, throwing me a curt, "I don't have time for you."

"No problem. I didn't come to see you. I came to see Sherri."

"Well, if you did want to see me, I wouldn't have time to talk to you now."

"And if you did have time, I wouldn't want to talk to you for more than five minutes anyway."

"I don't have five minutes."

"Good. Then, goodbye."

He stormed off. Minutes later, he was back, still gruff and scowling.

"What do you want to talk about? I can give you two minutes."

"Nothing. Go back to work."

"Come on. Two minutes. What do you want to say?"

"We'll talk about it another time."

"No. I'm here. What is it?" he demanded.

"Come outside."

We left the office.

"What?" he snapped.

"About the book—" That's as far as I got.

He erupted like a volcano. "No biography! Everybody wants to do a biography on me! No fucking biography! Peter Gent asked me to do a biography and I told him no! Simon and Schuster offered me two million for a biography and I told them no! Everybody wants to do a biography! No biography! That's it! None!"

I smiled at him.

He turned and stalked away.

"Hey," I called after him. "I've already told you: one way or another, I'm going to write about you."

So, this won't be a formal biography. Instead, it will be an intimate portrait of a complicated and extremely likable man, a superior acting talent, an intelligent man who is still tortured by life, though he strives constantly to understand himself and his relationship to others.

One

We were walking along Zuma Beach near his home in Malibu. Just the three of us: Nick, his nephew Eric Berg and I. The conversation had been light and playful. A lot of enjoyable teasing. Nick loves to tease, and Eric and I were giving as much as we were getting. Suddenly, things became a little serious. The subject had shifted to friendship.

"So," I said, "you've been out here how many years? Twenty-five? Thirty?"

"Yeah…about that," he answered.

"And you've made how many pictures now? Thirty-five? Forty?"

"Something like that."

"In all that time and through all that work, you've met thousands of people, right?"

"What're you getting at?"

"I just want to know how many friends you've made out here, that's all. How many?"

Silence settled over us as we walked.

He scuffed sand, he hunched his shoulders, he bent his head, and he pondered the question.

Long silence.

"Well, I'm waiting. How many?"

"I'm counting, I'm counting."

"What're you counting? Dozens?"

"More than that."

"You've made dozens of friends out here?"

"Hundreds."

"Okay, wait a second," I said. "Let's put some parameters around this. Let's get a friendship reference going for us."

"Like what?"

"Let's measure friendship against four considerations. Number one: A friend will never lie to a friend. He may color things a little to keep from hurting his friend, but he'll never lie to him."

"Okay," Nolte said, "I like that."

"Number two: A friend will never do anything intentionally to bring emotional or physical pain to a friend. He may do something inadvertently, but then he'll feel guilty as shit and never really get over the fact that he did it."

"That's a good one, too. What's the third?"

"A friend will be helpful to a friend. He can be counted on because he's interested and he cares."

"And the last one?"

"It's what the word means, and it circumscribes the other three. The word friend comes from German, and it means one who loves, a lover. If a friendship doesn't have love in it, it's not friendship. It could be association or acquaintance or any number of things, but it's not friendship. Now, using that as a reference, how many friends have you made out here in thirty years and in all your work?"

A long silence as we continued to walk.

"Well, I'm waiting. How many?"

"I'm counting, I'm counting."

Finally he stopped walking, and he looked at Eric and me. His face didn't wear his usual, engaging smile. His eyes were sadly serious.

"Well," he said, "using those four points as a guideline, I'd have to say three. I have three friends."

"That's it? Three friends? Who are they?"

"There's you—"

Actually, I've never been quite certain that we are friends. But I accepted the term then and answered, "No, no—I asked how many you've made out here. I don't count."

"Okay, then, two. There's Eric—"

"What're you doing? Eric's your nephew, for God's sake. He's family. You can't count him."

"Then there's just one—Billy Cross."

Billy Cross is a writer/actor with whom Nick has been close over the years.

"You mean, in all these years you've made only one real friend?"

He nodded and made a troubled face.

Now, the follow-up to this came three years later, when Nolte and I were spending a day together at his home in Fort Lauderdale, Florida. It was a day of continual laughter and meaningful discussion. Somehow, the subject of friendship came up again.

"Remember years ago, when you, Eric and I were walking along the beach and we were talking about this?" I asked.

He nodded. "Yeah, I remember."

"You said then, you had only one friend—Billy Cross."

His face clouded, and he shook his head. "Billy's no friend," he said abruptly.

"What happened?"

"He's no friend."

That's all he would say. I've never found out what happened to change that relationship. But something serious must have taken place to leave Nick Nolte totally friendless in Los Angeles.

Furthermore, though I don't know the particulars, I feel fairly certain that much of the responsibility belongs to Nick. Because the truth of his character is that Nolte may be incapable of the caring interest that's part of any friendship and, except for his son Brawley, of expressing the love that's necessary to sustain any meaningful relationship.

His first wife, Sheila, told me that years ago.

His last wife, Rebecca, said the same thing to me fairly recently.

And his present girlfriend, Vicki, shook her head as we stood in the kitchen of his Malibu estate, and murmured, "He's a tough one, all right."

"Hang in there, Vicki," I responded. "He loves you."

She seemed doubtful. "He does?"

I smiled. "He does."

"How do you know that?"

"He told me."

She brightened. "Thank you," she said. "That helps."

Later, I told Nick of this conversation. I expected him to warm to it and, perhaps, to approach Vicki tenderly about it. But he didn't. Instead, he frowned and grumbled, "We've been together more than four years, and she doesn't know I love her?"

Somehow, he feels that time, proximity and sex are sufficient indicators of love. He can't seem to understand that his women would welcome some genuine tenderness, appreciation and warm attention, as well.

In 1994, while Nick, Eric and I were in Paris for three months, Eric used to say very playfully about himself: "I'm deep, complex and mysterious."

We joked constantly about that and, because Nick is a recovering alcoholic, I gave him a cartoon that I'd found in a flea market: a picture of a boy holding a slew of wine bottles, and a man looking at him thirstily. The picture was titled *Nicolas*. Under the title, I printed *and Eric*. And then I added cartoon balloon dialogue.

For Nick: "You're not going to drink all that wine by yourself, are you?"

For Eric: "Yes. That's what makes me deep, complex and mysterious."

Today, the picture hangs in Nick's studio in Malibu, near his computer. He rarely looks at it, if ever. And it's not there because his relationship with Eric has been close and productive, nor as a sentimental reminder of our hilarious high jinks in France. (Unless he's drunk, Nick Nolte is light years away from sentimentality.) It's there, I believe, because that line *I'm deep, complex and mysterious* has a suggestive appeal to him. It should be his line, not Eric's. And though I've never heard him apply it to himself, I know he likes to think of himself that way: *deep, complex and mysterious.*

And what's even more interesting is the fact that he is.

Most people will be surprised by that assessment; many who believe they know him will disagree with it.

Bette Midler, for one, will certainly disagree. Nick prepared for his role in *Down and Out in Beverly Hills* by living among the homeless in Los Angeles flophouses. She became convinced that he was a self-serving slob, too dedicated to the realism of his character to appreciate the effect his stench and filth were having upon her and other members of the cast.

Julia Roberts will undoubtedly disagree. She wouldn't even do her off-camera lines for him when they were shooting his close-ups for *I Love Trouble.*

"Why?" I asked him.

"I don't know," he answered. "I don't know what I did to her. I even went into her trailer to apologize for whatever it was. I told her I'd accept full responsibility for it. But she started to hit me, and she threw me out, screaming, 'You're no man! You're weak! You're not a man!'"

"You're not a man? What the hell does that mean?"

"I don't know."

"Did you ever fuck her?"

"No."

"Did you try?"

"No. Maybe that's what it means. I dunno. She was weird."

And Barbra Streisand would probably say, "*Deep, complex and mysterious*? Nick Nolte? Don't make me laugh. More like shallow, fearful and non-supportive."

"How'd you get along with Streisand?" I asked when they had completed *Prince of Tides.*

"Fine."

"She a good director?"

"Very good. She knows just what she wants. But when she's acting, she's too self-conscious and she can't separate the director from the actor."

"What do you mean?"

"We were doing a love scene. And we were really going. All of a sudden, she says, 'Cut! That's it.' I said, 'What are you doing? We were just getting started. We could have had some good stuff there.' And she said,

'Whew! No, that's enough. I don't need anymore.' She's very sexy, but she couldn't stop directing and go for it like the actor."

"But you enjoyed working with her, right?"

"Yeah. It was good."

Then why would Streisand consider Nolte shallow, fearful and non-supportive? Because he wasn't there for her at Academy Award time. She wanted that Oscar desperately for her direction. She even called him to enlist his support in the pre-voting period, when nominees jockey for position with ads and interviews.

Nick turned her down.

"Why?" I asked him.

"Because I don't do that shit," he answered.

"But you've given interviews for *Prince of Tides*, and you're a Best Actor nominee."

"If the studio didn't force me, I wouldn't do it even for myself."

And that's true. He wouldn't. He's always preferred to do a film and then move on to the next project, divorcing himself from post-production hype, returning to his reclusive lifestyle without fanfare.

Deep, complex and mysterious?

I've known Nick Nolte for more than thirty years now and, believe me, that's accurate.

We met in Phoenix in the 1960's. I was forming an acting company with a friend and actor, Michael Byron. It was to be called Actors Inner Circle.

At the time, Nick was visiting his mother, Helen, who was operating a little antique business. He was introduced to me by another actor, Burke Rhind, one of the charter members of the group.

"I think you ought to meet this guy I just got to know," Burke had said. "He wants to be an actor. Doesn't have any experience, but the fire's there."

"Fire's what we'll need. Arrange it. We'll talk."

We met in a theater, where I was directing *Middle of the Night*, and we talked. I told him about our plans for an acting company with its own theater facility, and he told me all about his inexperience and his hunger to act. The fire was there, all right. Some people are wannabes, and some people are gottabes. It was evident from his opening words that he fit squarely and eternally into the gottabe category.

"Burke told me you're starting an acting company. I'd like to be part of it."

"You don't live in Phoenix."

"I'll move here."

"It's all freebie. We won't be paying in the beginning, if ever."

"I don't care."

"And since you don't have any experience, the parts may be small and disappointing."

"They'll get bigger."

"If you're good."

"I'll be good."

"At least four productions a year, long hours, heavy rehearsal schedules, and mandatory acting classes."

"That's terrific!"

He had more than eagerness and enthusism; he had need. I gave him a role in *Middle of the Night*, without even reading him for the part, and he did exceptionally well against his first leading lady, Gaye Hartwig (now Autterson), who later gained fame as the wonderful voice of Betty Rubble in *The Flintstones*. After that, Nolte joined Actors Inner Circle and became one of its mainstays, performing minor roles without complaint and major roles with stunning power and efficacy. He was indefatigable. He never tired of work or study.

We were all learning then, and Nick poured himself into the process with a vengeance. He took copious notes. He examined and discussed acting nuances with the intensity of a rabbinical scholar debating Torah. He reveled in the demanding and exhausting conduct of rehearsal. He created exciting moments onstage. And when critics and audiences responded favorably to his efforts, he used their reactions to hone his skills and talents even further. In short, he became the total actor. And it was all fun to him. Hard work but, nevertheless, great fun. He was interested in other things, of course, like photography and drawing. But nothing else interested him as much as his acting. Not even love, sex and, certainly, not marriage.

It was while he was with Actors Inner Circle that he married Sheila Paige, another member of the group and an equally exciting talent. They had met before the formation of the company. But during our production of Arthur Miller's *After the Fall*, they sneaked off into the serenity of the desert. Literally. They disappeared one afternoon into the desert near an architectural ruin called Shiprock. Alone there, they held hands, looked into each other's eyes and spoke their vows in the sight of God and the spirit of Frank Lloyd Wright. That night, they came to the theater and announced their "marriage."

The next day, they went to City Hall to make it official. But Nick had trouble with the formal commitment. They walked around the building four or five times while he tried to muster enough courage to enter. The courage wouldn't come. So they went home. About six weeks later, Nick finally informed Sheila that he was ready, that he was sure he wanted to do this. The marriage was quickly legalized before he could change his mind.

It was all so improbable. So romantic. But how long can romance survive when the groom is a confirmed alcoholic with a propensity for emotional violence? He never struck Sheila. Not physically. But his words often beat her more savagely than his fists ever could. Especially when he was drunk. When he was loaded, Nolte could become an abusive, demanding maniac whose unpredictability terrified his wife.

Sober, he saw himself as her teacher, and when she knew as much or more about life and acting as he, his reactions were often emotionally shattering. However, drunk or sober, he didn't take opposition easily.

Well, that hasn't changed. He's the same today, only more so. Oppose him on *any* intellectual point and his ability to listen gets short-circuited by his need to convince. This flagrant disregard for the opinions of others is directly related to his work.

Obsessive to the point of desperation, he throws himself so completely into preparing for his roles that nothing, absolutely *nothing*, may be considered too small for examination, especially the structure of an emotion.

"Jesus," he will exclaim, "don't dig so fucking deep into an idea unless it can lead me to an understanding of what I'm *feeling*! I work from emotion. I have to know why I'm feeling what I'm *feeling*. What's behind it? How is it expressed? What's its source? What's the emotional line?"

He will even agonize over a single word. "What's the meaning of the word *trim*?"

"Well, it has a few meanings. It can mean to make tidy or neat, like trimming a beard; it can mean to decorate, like trimming a Christmas tree; it can refer to the balance of a ship, or—"

"No, it's none of those. Jefferson says to his secretary, 'Well, my friend, you're in a pretty trim today.' What does he mean?"

"Oh, there it means mettle, spirit, being buoyant, like 'You're in a good mood today.'"

"I don't think so. It means more than that," he insisted.

"Like what?"

"I don't know. The line doesn't go anywhere if that's all it means. I have to understand it or I won't be able to keep an emotional hold on the scene. It has to lead me somewhere. The next line isn't connected to it."

"It's just an observation on Jefferson's part," I offered. "It's not meant to go anywhere."

"No. Ruth doesn't write that way. Find out what it means. Ask Jim; he'll know."

James Ivory, the director, offered the dictionary definition of the word. But the writer, Ruth Jhabvala, objected, saying it meant "mess" to her.

When Nick was told, he was elated. "That's it! You see, I knew there was more to it than you said!"

"But Jim had the same meaning as mine."

"Well, I said Jim wouldn't know either, didn't I? But you got it right from the writer. That's great!"

When reminded that the line could have come straight from Jefferson's writing, not Ruth's, his response was, "Well, yes, it could be Jefferson's, but she knows what she means. Now, I've got it. *Trim.* Now I know what it *really* means."

This need to know and always to be right goes beyond

an immediate screenplay. It goes into the heart of his work. He will consume everything he can get his hands on that is related to a role. If he's portraying an artist, he studies art; if he's a war veteran, he studies war; if he's a convict, he reads everything about our penal system; if he's Thomas Jefferson, he tries to absorb the entire Revolutionary period.

In discussions he rarely listens, rarely assimilates what he should be listening to. Instead, he reacts immediately to what he hears, using the other party as a springboard for the expression of his own ideas. These ideas and opinions are often interesting and valid. But at the same time, they're often superficial, lacking life experience. Because his work is almost exclusively his life, he truly believes his film experience is life experience. For example, he once said: "Picasso wasn't such a good artist. I was talking to Trumbull the other day, and he told me he went to the Picasso Museum. He wasn't impressed with Picasso, either."

Now, Trumbull's statement was supposed to give support to Nick's own negative opinion about Picasso. And he seemed genuinely surprised when reminded that Trumbull was really Nigel, a young actor from London, and that being an artist in the film, *Jefferson in Paris*, in no way made Nigel's statements about Picasso valid.

"I know," he replied lamely, with a sheepish smile, "but he's Jefferson's artist."

He realized his position had been ridiculous and that it had made him look foolish. It bothered him, but he changed the subject quickly rather than admit his folly. However, months later, still dogged by the memory of the moment, he found an opportunity to say, "Remember when I said Picasso was a lousy artist? Shit, I never really believed that. I just said it to get a confrontation going and to stir my juices."

The truth is, having played a painter in Martin Scorsese's segment of *New York Stories*, Nolte believes he became qualified to judge Picasso; having played a disturbed southerner in *Prince of Tides*, he has become an authority on the dysfunctional family and Piedmont and Tidewater geography; having played a Viet Nam vet in *Who'll Stop the Rain?* has made him an authority on the entire 60's social revolution; having played a bum in *Down and Out in Beverly Hills* has given him incontestable insights into the homeless; and having played Thomas Jefferson, he's now comfortable with ideas and opinions on democracy, monarchy, slavery and love.

He's made more than forty motion pictures; his investigations have covered a lot of territory: politics, art, law and order, literature, education, medicine, sports, ideology, psychology, journalism, bigotry, and a host of other subjects. Voracious reading in all those areas has forged strong convictions. He believes he's done more than his share of homework to reach his understanding. Therefore, anyone who hasn't done an equal amount of investigation can't possibly know as much as he. As a result, he becomes short-tempered and vociferous whenever he's challenged by an opposing view. A challenge triggers immediate reaction and leaves no room for discussion. He will not listen patiently and exchange ideas; he will talk over the other person's words, become louder and louder, increasingly intense, with his face contorted, spit flying, arms flailing the air, and, finally, he may shout in anger and frustration, "No, listen to me! Listen to me, goddammit! You're not listening to me!"

Most of the time, he overwhelms his opposition with

this behavior. But not always.

While making *Blue Chips* with Billy Friedkin directing, Nolte went into one of these outbursts, and started to shout while trying to make his point. Billy's soft comment was, "Nick, I know how to shout, too."

Whereupon they conducted a screaming match that lasted about ten minutes. After Billy walked away, Nolte felt hurt. He sulked for a while, but he did the scene the way Friedkin wanted and rationalized his capitulation by saying it was what he'd intended all along; there had just been a breakdown in communication.

Except for the added years, Nick Nolte, in many ways, is the same funny, charming and intense person today that he was when he learned to act in Actors Inner Circle. People used to say then, he was capable of anything wild and crazy, but when they said that, the statement was usually couched in warmth and appreciation. He was a free spirit. From doing drugs and booze in the desert to jumping on couches naked at parties to stripping during rehearsals to reveling in group sex with other members of the company. He wanted no restrictions whatsoever upon his behavior, no limitations to his search for freedom. He was undisciplined, and he hated demands made upon him. But when it came to his acting, he was a totally committed artist. He never missed a rehearsal or a performance. Never failed to learn his lines quickly. Never came to the theater drunk, or tripped-out on peyote or LSD. Never opposed direction or challenged company authority. And, most important, he never lost his playfulness and his wonderful sense of humor. He was a director's dream. And, if his respect can be gained, he still is a director's dream. Nevertheless, one of our actors often called him a perennial teenager, predicting he would never grow up. And one of his women confirmed that prediction recently in telling me, "He's still an adolescent. Nothing will ever change him."

That's not quite accurate, of course. There have been changes. Significant changes. Half a lifetime in Hollywood has taken its toll.

So, what is he today? What is his outlook on life? How does he work? How does he relate to others? What are his demons? The answers to these questions can be understood best by the many wonderful, fascinating and even crazy things he did and said during the ten months we worked together on *Jefferson in Paris*.

Two

"I've just been offered something interesting. But I'm not sure I want to do it."

"What is it?" I asked.

"Thomas Jefferson."

"That is interesting. Who's directing and producing?"

"James Ivory's directing. Ismail Merchant's producing. You want to read the script?"

"If you want me to."

"I'll have Sherri send you a copy."

Sherri UPSed the manuscript immediately.

After reading it, I called him. "Nicholas."

"Yeah?"

"I've read the screenplay. It's good."

"You think so?"

"Do it. You'll be Jefferson, man."

"I liked it, too. Very much. But I don't know. That'll be four pictures back-to-back. I need a break."

He was tired. Dead tired. But Nolte chooses his films on the basis of only two considerations: one, whether or not he can learn something that will help him to know himself better, and two, whether the director is respected for the quality of his work. Money plays absolutely no part in his decision.

Once, when he'd finished work on *Blue Chips*, in which he played an abrasive and totally unappealing basketball coach, he explained his acceptance of the role to me with, "The guy's crazy—off-the-wall obsessive. *I'm* crazy—off-the-wall obsessive. I figured if I could learn something about *his* craziness, I'd know something about *mine*. And Billy Friedkin was directing."

And I was with him when Jim Wiatt, then his agent, called to inform him he'd just been offered $13,000,000 to do a film. Remember, this was long before the $20,000,000 Jim Carrey breakthrough when thirteen million was the top figure for superstars. Nick turned the project down without hesitating.

"Why'd you turn it down?" I asked.

"There's nothing in it. And nobody's directing."

"They're offering you thirteen million and they don't have a name director?"

"Nobody I'd care to work with."

"But that's a lot of money for a few months work."

"Fuck it."

So, with highly respected James Ivory at the helm and the third president of the United States as his mentor, exhausted or not, Nolte agreed to go directly into his fourth production for one-eighth his usual fee.

He was doing a musical, *I'll Do Anything*, when he accepted the Jefferson role. James Brooks was directing. Rock star Prince had written the music, and Twyla Tharp was choreographing the dance numbers.

"You sing like a banshee and dance like a three-legged elephant with a bad case of diarrhea," I said with a laugh. "What the hell are you doing in a musical?"

He laughed also. "Damned if I know. I wanted to

work with Brooks. He's a fine director. He knows I can't sing or dance, so I'm talking my songs, and Twyla's making it look like I'm dancing. It's a good script. I had to test for the part. Can you imagine?"

"Why?"

"James was afraid I was too old for it."

"Were you?"

"Yeah. They tried to make me look younger. Pulled my face back behind my ears. You should have seen me. I was stretched so tight when I smiled, I thought I'd split down the middle. I looked like a mummy."

"So, why'd they give you the part?"

"They liked my read—enough for them to make the character older. So with a lot less stretching and a little more age adjustment, I told James, I could make it work."

But nothing could make that film work. It was a disaster from day one. And when audiences actually booed it during previews, the studio decided to drop it as a musical and to throw more money into it to make it a slight romantic comedy.

Nick's reaction to this was typical Nolte. He rationalized the failure, continued to idealize the concept, blamed the studio, and denied preview audience responses. As far as he was concerned, James Brooks was a genius who could have made it work if he'd only been given the chance.

Though he is wonderfully astute in all matters concerning the acting process, Nolte also has a remarkable capacity for self-delusion. It's as if he's incapable of admitting an association with failure, as if such an admission diminishes him, personally, not his talent, but his very being.

This was the situation: after *I'll Do Anything*, he would do *I Love Trouble* with Julia Roberts. At the same time, he'd be looping *I'll Do Anything* and preparing to go directly into Merchant Ivory's *Jefferson in Paris*.

Obviously, there would be no time for the necessary research into Jefferson's character and the Revolutionary era. He had reason to be concerned.

"Nick, you're up to your ass now. I've always been interested in Jefferson. This is one I'd like to help you with. I'll do the historical research, and then we'll work together on character analysis and script interpretation."

"Really?"

"It'll be fun. Like the old days."

"Great!"

Nick never approaches a role half-heartedly. Now with the burden of research lifted, he was tremendously relieved.

"How do you want to approach it?" he asked.

"I think a trip to Virginia and Washington, D.C. is necessary," I said. "Monticello, Williamsburg, William and Mary College, the University of Virginia, the Library of Congress, maybe some plantations."

"How long will you need?"

"Five days."

"When do you want to go?"

"I'm flexible, but soon."

"Great. I'll check my schedule. We'll go together. Eric will go with us."

"That'll be perfect!"

Besides being Nolte's nephew, Eric was his assistant. He was twenty-seven then. Quick-witted, with a razor tongue and a strangely engaging cynical attitude, his inexhaustible spirit in the face of innumerable problems always allowed the actor part of Nick to concentrate exclusively on any role he happened to be playing. With Eric there to buffer him, there was never really anything to worry Nolte except his work.

"I'll have Sherri arrange things as soon as I see when I can get away," he said. "I'm really excited about this now."

His happiness could be heard in the lift of his voice. When he's enthusiastic, that gravelly pitch rises noticeably and almost rings with laughter.

Our five days in Virginia and Washington proved to be an extremely significant beginning. However, though there was a wealth of information on the background of Thomas Jefferson, Nick was unhappy by the absence of the man.

"Sure," he said, "we get a feel of history, but we don't get a feel of Jefferson himself. I have to know the emotional power of the man."

There it was again, the need to grasp passions.

What made the trip valuable? Not the feel of the man, which was missing, but the feel of eighteenth century southern life, which was everywhere. The Shirley Plantation, with its reconstructed slave quarters; the Carter Grove Plantation, preserved in eighteenth century splendor; Monticello, with its glorious perfection; and Williamsburg, where the past permeates everything from the Governor's Palace to the town jail.

Nolte believes he can grasp a man's feelings if he understands his environment. So, there were questions and more questions, a thousand questions, for the guides who had been assigned to help us. What time did people go to sleep then? What did they eat? How did they prepare their food? How did they set their tables? What was their entertainment? What dances did they do? What games did they play? How often did they bathe? Did they brush their teeth? Yes? What were toothbrushes made of? How often did they change their clothes? Did they wear underwear? What did women use during their menstrual periods? What were kitchens like? What were mattresses made of? Did beds have springs? Did shoes have left and right feet? Where did their paper come from? What did people drink? Did they boil their water? What were the common diseases? How long did people live? How many hours in a work day? Was there toilet paper? No? Then what happened after defecation?

And when Linda Hamrick, an extraordinary guide, dressed Nick in an eighteenth century coat and hat and walked him through a popular dance step of the period, in the Apollo Room of the Raleigh Tavern where Jefferson had actually danced that same dance, Nolte began to feel the sense of a real person within the Jeffersonian legend. Nothing clear. Nothing defined. Merely the slightest sense of a Jefferson reality. But it was something, the emotional handle this actor always needs so desperately in his work.

The clerk at Colonial Williamsburg's bookstore nearly went out of her mind when he bought a copy of almost every book, pamphlet, audio and video cassette the shop had in stock.

"This should get us started," Nick said with a grin as Eric calculated how he would transport everything back to Malibu.

Nick didn't actually believe he could read, view and listen to everything he had purchased; he knew the demands of *I Love Trouble* would preclude that possibility. Then why did he buy almost everything in the bookstore?

Just to have it. In case a question about Jefferson and the Revolutionary period should arise that required an immediate answer. This would be his private library, his personal reference section, his bibliographical security blanket.

As it developed, his interest in the material became so profound that he actually tried to absorb all of it. And by the time he went before the cameras for *Jefferson in Paris*, he was versed enough in eighteenth century American history to have lectured on it to any high school or college class.

Leaving the bookstore, Nolte was on a happiness high. When everything seems to be proceeding the way he should like it to go, Nick usually becomes wild and unpredictable. He laughs with infectious glee and jokes in an engagingly teasing manner, often erupting suddenly in some ribald act that's intended to embarrass others.

This time I became the unsuspecting object of his cheerfulness. I was carrying books to our rented car when he sneaked up behind me and suddenly yanked my pants down to my knees. This sent him and Eric into paroxysms of laughter. I laughed, too, and calmly put my books down to rearrange myself.

"You're embarrassed!" Nick shouted.

"You can't embarrass me, Nick."

"You're embarrassed. Admit it, you're embarrassed."

Smiling, I acted superior. "I'm above embarrassment." And to reinforce the pose, I dropped my pants to my knees again, whereupon Nolte's head jerked quickly to his right and his left to see if anyone had observed me.

"Now, *you're* embarrassed."

"No, I'm not," he protested.

"Sure you are, or you wouldn't have looked around that way."

He likes to believe that, despite his stardom, he's still a liberated spirit, capable of outrageous statements and behavior. And he is. But that's only when his words and actions disconcert others. When he is not the initiator, his star-image can be threatened, and he reacts accordingly. Even with embarrassment.

This star-image is something Nolte doesn't wear lightly or easily. He feels it's a burden, something he's stuck with, something that follows him everywhere except into the privacy of his home.

Nick loves to walk. Whenever he can, he takes long walks, often restricting them to side streets when he's in a city, and to lonely stretches of beach or forest when he's in a more natural setting.

One day, in Washington, we went on an early morning walk. Except for the homeless, the streets were relatively empty at that hour. However, passing a grassy hillock with its brick planter, we suddenly heard a voice calling loudly from the top of the hill, "Hey, Nick! Hey, man! Hey, Nolte!"

Nick looked up at the caller.

A ragged, bearded man waved his arms and actually jumped up and down. "Hey, you're Nolte, aincha? Yeah? Hey, Nick!"

Nick waved a hand, bowed his head and kept on walking.

"Hey, man, I seen your picture—with Eddie Murphy—you're terrific, man…you're great…I love ya…."

Nick shook his head and snorted.

About twenty feet away, a bedraggled woman sat on the planter, watching the man on the hill and our approach. When we reached her, she spat sourly, "Who the fuck do you think *you* are? You're nobody. That's who you are, you're *nobody*!"

Nolte smiled at me. "Either way, I lose," he said.

There are times, though, when recognition works to his advantage, and he doesn't seem to mind that at all. The special attention we received from our guides. Access to restricted areas, like the excavations going on under the Capitol building. The restricted stacks of the Library of Congress, where original historical documents are kept. He will accept all special attention when that preferential treatment is related to his work or to some other on-going interest.

For example, though he's basically a pacifist, Nolte is almost pathologically fascinated by violence. He now believes it to be genetically rooted in the male animal. The idea came to him while preparing for his role in *Affliction*. And he will quote sections eagerly from one of his research sources, *Demonic Males* by Wrangham and Peterson, to support his contention.

Well, in the last hours of our five-day investigation into Jefferson's American roots, he said "We've got five hours to kill before we go to Dulles Airport. What'll we do?"

"We said we'd come back someday and visit the Holocaust Museum," I offered. "How about doing that now?"

He brightened at the suggestion. Nazi violence? Absolutely. It was right in line with a major interest.

"Yeah. Let's do it."

Now, ordinarily, Nolte hates anyone's using his celebrity to gain an advantage. Jokingly, I once said I might take out an ad in the *Hollywood Reporter*, identifying myself as his acting coach. He didn't see the humor in that, and he actually protested apprehensively. He'll even berate Brawley for identifying himself as Nick Nolte's son. However, there was no objection whatsoever when I asked a guard at the museum, "Do you recognize that man standing all by himself over there?"

The line of people waiting to enter was endless.

"That's Nick Nolte, the actor, isn't it?"

"That's right. Look, we have to leave Washington in a few hours, and we'd like to see as much of the museum as possible before we head for Dulles. Would that be possible, please?"

After a moment's hesitation, a rope was lowered, and we slipped into a side entrance.

Nolte went through the museum without communicating a word of thought or feeling. But, later, walking toward our car, head bent, deep in concentration, Nick broke his long silence with a painful groan.

"Jesus, that was incredible!" he said. "Someday, we have to do something on hatred. Not just violence—on the hatred that's behind it. Where it comes from. What it's all about."

"You mean, dissect it—get at its roots? Something on the anatomy of hatred?"

"Yeah. We must."

The Holocaust Memorial Museum had devastated him.

He never regretted how we had gained admittance. It was just another instance of someone's favor serving one of his interests. In a quiet way, and without even thinking about it, he simply accepted and appreciated what his celebrity had done for him.

Three

The next seven months became a period of intense preparation.

"Okay, how do you want to do this?" he asked.

"I'll go back to Phoenix and work there for a couple of weeks, and then come out here and we can go over what I discover."

"How long will you be able to stay?"

"As long as necessary."

"Great. I'll have the guest house ready for you, and someone'll pick you up at the airport."

"Perfect. We'll keep doing it that way—two weeks at home and two weeks here with you, until we nail it."

And, for the most part, that's how it went. Sometimes we'd work together for three weeks at a time, sometimes for only a week or ten days. But the schedule took on a rhythm that permitted Nick to immerse himself in the process with no damage to his involvement in *I Love Trouble*.

The damage there came from his relationship with Julia Roberts.

"I think she's nuts," he would say. "Even the directors think so. She pulls her star shit whenever she can."

"Like what? Give me an example."

"Like, in one scene, I'm being choked and bent backwards over a rail. She's supposed to save me by hitting the guy with a gun. So, she does the bit, but her hand touches the guy's head. I mean, it just *touched* him. You should have seen her. She acted like she broke her whole arm. She had everybody going crazy, running around, looking for an ice pack. Then, another time, she said she hurt her ankle, and she had people actually carry her onto the set."

"Would you work with her again?"

"Never."

Now, this is particularly interesting, because, though he deplores star temperament in others, Nolte's not exactly free of the disease himself. Of course, he never sees his own erratic displays in that light. There's always justification for his actions. It's either that someone's not giving him the attention he thinks he needs and deserves, or his understanding of something is not really being appreciated, or it could be dissatisfaction with what he judges to be incompetence in others, or simply disappointment in the attitudes of his fellow actors. But, whatever it is, to Nick's credit, he never pulls the kind of self-pitying stunts he ascribed to Julia Roberts. Instead, his temperamental displays are restricted on the set to the rare outburst, which is supposed to drive home an important point, or to silly little demands that are supposed to ease the enormous pressure he always believes he's under.

The guest house on Nick's estate is a three-car garage affair, with two bathrooms, a fully appointed kitchen, a huge living room, a large bedroom with a grand bed that requires steps to get into, and two other rooms, in which, at that time, he kept all his tanning equipment.

The estate itself is large, with a marvelous main house and three other houses besides the guest house. One was used by the family of his gardener, Herrado. Another housed Nolte's extensive gymnasium. The last was Nick's studio where we did much of the preparation for the Jefferson role. In addition to the buildings, the property has an extensive vegetable garden and even a rabbit hutch, not to mention the obligatory tennis court and swimming pool. And recently it was augmented beautifully by the purchase of his neighbor's property.

"She wanted a million-eight for it," he said. "I offered one-four."

"Cash?"

"Of course." In his mind, a million-four was just a piece of film, a few weeks' work, not really money. "I'll take out the fence and use the main house there as a studio for myself and an office for Sherri."

"What'll you do with the present studio?"

"It'll be a playhouse for Brawley and his friends. C'mon, lemme show you the new grounds. They're beautiful. All kinds of flowers and fruit trees. Wait'll you see them."

There's something about nature that touches Nolte deeply. Maybe it's that nature doesn't impose itself upon him. He accepts it on its terms, and enjoys the respect it shows him. In the quiet of nature, he can forget the whole crazy business of making motion pictures. He can ease himself into the restful, introspective moods that are at the core of his persona. Nature nurtures him. Truly. It feeds his soul. He can marvel at the bloom of a flower. He can delight in the flavor of a berry picked off a vine. He can gush at the contours of a huge tree. And his property is filled with these things, always stirring deep, honest feelings, always enriching him. If there were only two people alive on this planet who truly loved their homes, one would surely be Nick Nolte.

And he enjoys sharing it. A guest on the Nolte estate has free run of the place. All doors are open to him. The kitchen is his. Cars are at his disposal. Even Nick's clothes are his. Nolte places no restrictions on his hospitality.

However, this generosity is available only to those who serve an immediate purpose. He's refused me the use of his guest house a number of times. And that's because he didn't have any needs at the time that my presence could satisfy. These needs don't have to be professional. They can be social, as well. When he's alone and wants company, he's open and responsive.

Until recently, Nick owned a house in Fort Lauderdale. A B-I-I-G house. The first time I saw it, I called it a labyrinth. I don't know how many rooms it had, but one could get lost going from room to room until becoming acquainted with the layout. It was a two-story affair, with an elevator that didn't work, and the barest of furnishings in all the rooms.

"Are you going to fix the place up?" I asked.

"No. I really don't need it. It's just a place to stay when I want to visit Brawley."

His son lived with his mother, Rebecca, about a dozen houses down the street.

I stayed there one night with Nick while I was in Florida on some family matters. He welcomed my company eagerly; he'd been in Fort Lauderdale more than a month, and he felt relatively alone and lonely. We had a great time together. But when I said I'd like to use the house for a couple of days sometime, while he's in California or away on a shoot, the answer was a quick, "No."

No one would be using it. Nothing would be harmed by my stay. But the answer was still, "No." Why? Because that's Nolte: unless coerced, he will never agree to anything that doesn't benefit him directly. Not even for a friend. And he doesn't do this selfishly from an unwillingness to share. Because, in truth, Nolte can be magnanimous to the point of extravagance without the slightest concern for the cost. Rather, his negativism is an automatic response directly related to a deep-seated fear of being used. And this fear asserts itself whenever there are no immediate needs to be satisfied.

In our months together on the *Jefferson* film, Nick never felt used. Instead, he felt he was being helped and, for this, he was openly grateful. Consequently, plane tickets were always ready. Limousines were always waiting. The guest house was always prepared. One of his Mercedes was always available. The slightest request was always honored without a moment's hesitation. His entire demeanor was gracious and affable at all times, despite the horrendous experience of *I Love Trouble* and the weight and demands of *Jefferson in Paris* preparation.

And that preparation was, indeed, heavy and unrelenting.

When he wasn't actually before the *I Love Trouble* cameras, he devoted every available moment to reading something about Thomas Jefferson and to putting his thoughts into his computer.

A few words about this computer because it has become a lifeline to his art. He will spend endless hours at the machine, scanning material into it, extrapolating pertinent elements, creating special files, building the essential reference that will lead him to the heart of his character. It is the most up-to-date instrument that his money can buy. As soon as a new computer feature appears on the market, Nolte acquires it. Nothing that can help him to understand his work better is allowed to escape his attention. And a personal computer specialist is ready at all times to keep him abreast of the latest technological developments and to devise new programs that will sharpen his acting skills further and allow ever-deeper penetration into the soul of his characters.

And that is what he is after. Always. The soul of a character.

To get at that soul, Nolte needs mental images. All information is used to conjure pictures, and these pictures produce the understanding that leads him to his essential emotional line.

Every night, before a roaring fire in the living room of the main house, with Nick sprawled on one large couch and me on a couch facing him across a huge table, we'd drink gallons of hot lemonade and carefully consider the life of Thomas Jefferson, trying to find the soul of the man within the dead elements of historical fact.

"I have to see him," Nick would say. "How did he stand? How did he walk? How did he sit? What did he sound like? How did he think? What were his emotional reactions? What was he like?"

To answer the multitudinous questions that beset him, we used a clearly defined process of inquiry that has been the foundation of his skills from the earliest days of his acting career. First, we read the screenplay aloud. He read all of Jefferson's speeches; I read all other dialogue, and we shared author descriptions and directions. We read slowly, carefully, only a few pages each night, making detailed notes related to glimpses of Jefferson's character on the basis of what he says, what he does, what is said to him, what is done to him, and what is said about him. Every line was interpreted in an effort to find corresponding adjectives. When Jefferson said, "Alas, my duties were official or I would have returned weeks ago," the adjective "dedicated" was placed near the speech; when he lifted his little daughter and kissed her, the words "gentle and loving" were added; when directions said he pulled himself together, we wrote "controlled, collected." In this way, by the time the entire screenplay had been examined, Nolte had a long list of adjectives that allowed him to see Jefferson's character at a glance.

According to the scenario (to demonstrate this phase of Nick's process with only a few of the collected adjectives) Thomas Jefferson was a *dedicated* man, a *loving, gentle* man, a man who was *controlled, disciplined* and *restrained*, a *witty*, and *gracious* man, whose *intellectual* and *creative* powers were extraordinary. He was also a *sensitive, proud* and *demanding* man driven by an unassailable belief in the American Ideal and a covenant that he'd made with his daughter, Patsy. This became the foundation of further examination.

The screenplay was read carefully again and again, and each time, every single line was probed at length in respect to its place in the *action* of the story. For example, in one scene, Jefferson is discussing his Declaration of Independence with some French liberal aristocrats, and he's challenged by Lafayette about the absence of property in the "unalienable" rights sentence "...that among these are life, liberty and the pursuit of happiness." Jefferson responds by saying he believes property may *lead* to happiness but that property isn't an end in itself.

Next to the line, we wrote: "The debate is being setup. The notion of *property* is to be the *main* point of their discussion. The liberals are concerned about the loss of *their* property. To them, that's more important than the slavery issue."

When Jefferson begs Maria, his great love, to meet with him again and she tells him that she wishes she could, we wrote: "She knows that a life with him would be possible only on her romantic terms; he'd have to stay in France and give up his ideals of liberty and equality, which he could never do. *That* much she understands."

And while this phase of investigation proceeded, Nolte immersed himself in the historical and biographical facts of Jefferson's life.

Endless discussions took place to connect these facts with Jefferson's character in the film.

"How the hell can he talk so much about the equality of all men and still own two hundred slaves back in America?" Nolte agonized. "I have to have an answer. If I don't have an answer, I'll feel like a hypocrite. And Jefferson *wasn't* a hypocrite. He was sincere. So I have to understand how he can feel sincere and still practice something that he was against. If I don't understand that sincerity, I'll never be able to feel it. And if I don't *feel* it, it'll never come out honestly. So, what's the answer?"

"There is no answer. People have been trying to explain that contradiction for more than a hundred years."

"But I've gotta have an answer or everything I say is bullshit! Let's make up something that can satisfy *me*."

So, we created three explanations based on fact, and Nick chose one.

It was: slavery until very recent history was not considered an evil or a social injustice. It had been an integral part of numerous sophisticated societies where slaves constituted a distinct class with specific legal rights. In Jefferson's Virginia, though slaves had no legal rights, slavery was still respectable and just coming into question. Jefferson, while questioning it, was still part of that respectability. So, viewed from the perspectives of eighteenth century slavery respectability and twentieth century civil rights sensibilities, Jefferson is caught in the middle. On the one hand, he accepts the practice of the day because he's truly a man of his Age; on the other, he questions the principle of slavery because he's definitely a man of the future.

Comfortable with that, Nolte was able to move on. That's another thing about Nick. He must always feel comfortable with what he's doing. Everything must fit neatly into its place. There may be no holes. No unanswered questions. Holes and questions breed *dis*comfort, and discomfort feeds his enormous self-doubts.

At another time, he said: "Jesus, they really beat the shit out of him during the Revolution, when he was governor of Virginia. They actually brought him up on charges of incompetence and cowardice. And his wife and kids were dying all around him. He even told Washington he felt like a decrepit old man. So what does all of this mean to him while he's in France? With all of that inside me, how can I have this hot affair with Maria Cosway a little after I get to Paris, and then dump her a few months later and start to fuck my slave, Sally Hemings, who's only a fifteen-year-old kid, f'r Chrissake?! What the hell's the matter with me? What am I *thinking?!*"

At one point in the work, Nick said, "Okay, now we start The Book. I'll have Eric type up all our notes. Three copies. One for you, one for him, and one for me. Each of us should have a copy of The Book, don't you think?"

"Right."

The Book is Nolte's bible. He has developed one for every character he's ever portrayed in each of his films. It contains every bit of relevant work done in his research. Every insight is in it. Every pertinent fact. Every hypothesis. It contains the screenplay, the scene breakdowns, the character analysis, the known facts, the fictionalized back-stories. Everything. It is indispensable to his work. And it keeps growing. Always. By the end of principal photography, when those precious, happy words ring out, "Okay people, that's a final wrap," The Book may total more than a thousand pages.

It certainly did for *Jefferson in Paris*.

One of the most important parts of The Book is the section devoted to back-storying. In order to feel secure, Nolte must have the unwritten history of his character. Creating this with him is always challenging and great fun.

"Jefferson loved his father," he said. "You know what I need? I need something that describes the whole relationship, something that shows me all of Jefferson's thoughts, all his feelings, about what Peter did on his own and what, maybe, they did together."

We concocted a four page exposition of admiration, respect and love—one that detailed imaginary father-son activities intermingled with known facts.

"This is great," Nick said. "But it's not strong enough."

To make it stronger we put it into first person singular and made it a Jefferson monologue.

"This is better," Nick said, "but I still don't get the feel of it."

We worked on it again. We sharpened images. We

used more colorful adjectives, more dynamic verbs, and we contemporized the language without completely abandoning the flavor of eighteenth-century speech. Then we taped it, and it worked. It gave Nolte the necessary pictures on which he could build his emotional line.

"This is great!" Nick exulted. "I can see them, now. I understand what they must have meant to each other! I can feel Jefferson's love!"

A point is reached in his work when he believes his information must be personalized for him. It's the disconnected shooting of film, the absence of sequential work, that makes this necessary, he's convinced.

Actually, the depth of his investigation supplies him with all the continuity he needs, and a slight refresher before going in front of the cameras should be enough to get him going. But, the fact is, Nolte is *never* secure, even with this personalized step.

And at another time he said thoughtfully, "You know what I need? I need a letter from his daughter, Patsy, something that tells him she's going to become a Catholic. I'll get his emotional reaction if I can actually see the words."

Things like this happened so often that Eric once said, "Be grateful he's not playing a rock or he'd want the whole story of how he came to be formed, what prehistoric fossils live inside him, and why God didn't make him a tree!"

Nolte is not a hypochondriac. However, in recent years, he's developed an intense interest in his health and the condition of his body. He works out with fair regularity, though he's still a little soft and not nearly as strong as his size suggests. His refrigerator, freezer and cupboards are filled with health foods. He cooks huge amounts of excellent pastas and tasty soups, leaving leftovers in their pots on the stove and his dirty dishes all over the house, to be refrigerated or washed by anyone who finally finds the disorder too much to endure.

"Why don't you wash that glass?" Vicki asked him in exasperation.

"I'm not finished with it," he answered.

"There's nothing in it. Do you want it filled again?"

"No."

"Then, what do you mean, you're not finished with it?"

"Well, I drank out of this side. If I imagine the rim has four sides, I still have three more to go before it has to be washed."

"Give me that!" Vicki snapped, and she began to wash the glass and all the other dishes.

Nick grinned and winked as he passed me to go into the living room.

Nolte's not innately sloppy or dirty. He keeps his person surprisingly clean. He bathes every day. He wears fresh clothes more often than most people change their underwear. And he's acutely aware of what real slovenliness is. He's just indifferent. Domestic disarray simply doesn't bother him. It's as if there are too many other things, more important things, to absorb his interest. If his indifference bothers others—well, he's quite content to let them clean up for him.

One thing that does absorb his interest is his physical condition. He tracks himself periodically through indepth blood tests. These identify the level of every vitamin, mineral, enzyme, hormone and acid in his body.

The reports, which he studies assiduously, fill dozens of pages. They indicate perfect levels and where he stands in each category in relation to that perfection. This has produced a strict regimen that has him popping almost thirty pills a day, all in scientifically determined dosages, to achieve what can be, only in theory, a balanced endocrine system. Small bags of pills litter his kitchen counter, always in view and within easy reach, lest he forget to consume his daily prescriptions. Why this inordinate interest in his health? Why now? Clearly, to make up for lost time. Through most of his life, Nick was a dissolute fool. He will admit that readily. Interviews have made it common knowledge. Booze. Drugs. The worst kinds of food, when he ate at all. Long periods of sleeplessness. Utter disregard for the consequences of his lifestyle and its effect upon those close to him. He lived a gutter existence.

"But one day, I hit bottom," he told me. "I was so low, I knew I'd die if I didn't get help. It was like a scream. AA saved me. All along, I was full of my own shit. I thought I was in control of my life. I drank because I wanted to. I went where I went because I wanted to. I did everything because I wanted to. But, finally, I understood I had nothing to do with it. The booze was in control, not me. Everything that happened was dictated by the booze. When I realized that I wasn't in control of my life, I lost it, man. I became desperate and hollow. And there was nothing inside me but pain. Incredible pain. That's when the scream came, and that's when I went into Twelve Step. I know now, you gotta believe in something bigger than yourself or you die."

Now, with that kind of thinking, one might believe Nick Nolte has finally pulled his act together, and that he's achieved his deeply desired peace-of-mind. No such thing. Why? Because one of Nick's tragic weaknesses is an uncontrollable tendency to blow things out of proportion. If he's affected negatively by an experience, he doesn't step back and examine the situation. He broods, he agonizes, he wallows in his emotions. Reasoning with him becomes impossible. It's as if a wall goes up, behind which the problem festers. Inevitably, there are consequences to this kind of behavior. Sometimes, very frightening consequences.

"I'm scared," he confessed toward the start of our work in Malibu.

"About what?" I thought he was expressing his customary doubt about succeeding in his role.

"I've got PVC."

"What the hell's PVC? Post-Venereal Complications?"

"Premature Ventricular Contractions. There's something wrong with my heart."

"Jesus—what is it?"

"I don't know. It races and then it misses beats. It just started last week. Sometimes, it stops altogether. And I have to hit my chest to make it start again. Scares the shit out of me."

"What are you doing for it?"

"Beating myself black and blue."

"I mean medications, idiot. Are you taking any?"

"Yeah, but they don't help."

"What's causing it?"

"*I Love Trouble.* My divorce. I don't know how to reach Julia, and Rebecca's making things difficult. I try to talk to Julia, but she won't even look at me now. It's very unpleasant. It's affecting the work. As for Rebecca— Jesus, I thought we had it all worked out. But then the lawyers got into it, and her friends are always telling her to get this and take that. So, she's never satisfied. I don't know what the hell's gonna happen there. The doctor says PVC comes from pressure, and there's nothing to worry about. Easy for him to say. He doesn't have to deal with two women at the same time who hate him, and he's not the one whose heart is stopping. Jefferson could really kill me, y'know."

"Jefferson won't kill you. Jefferson'll bring you back to life."

And work on *Jefferson in Paris* really was his life saver.

Nolte loves the uncomplicated give-and-take of collaborative investigation. If he respects his coworker, he relaxes and enjoys himself completely, allowing his mind to fly in the most wonderful, unexplored directions.

"Do you think Jefferson notices Maria that first time, when she comes into Lafayette's party with her husband?" he asked one night near the fire.

"He'd have to. Her husband enters like a screaming banshee," I answered.

"I don't think he notices her."

I was surprised. "What are you talking about? Read the author's directions."

"I've read the directions. I don't care. I don't think he notices her."

"He can't help but notice her. The directions tell us the Cosways are announced and that her husband shrieks even louder than Lafayette. He's shrill. Even the way he dresses is loud. How could Jefferson *not* notice him? And since Maria's with him, he'd have to see her, too."

"I don't think so!" he insisted. " I think Jefferson's not even looking at them! I think he's busy talking to the scientists! He's not interested in some fop who's making a grand entrance!"

"The noise alone would have to attract him."

"No, no, no! He *can't* notice her now!"

"He has to. What is he, deaf? Blind?"

"He *can't!* If he notices her now, then he can't ignore her at the dinner table the way he does! He'll seem arrogant! Like she's not worth his attention! Then I lose the emotional moment when he *does* turn to her! He becomes interested in her! *That's* when he notices her! *That's* when he has to see her for the first time! He can't become interested if he sees her when she first comes in and then doesn't think she's worth his attention when she sits down next to him!"

He argued his point on his feet, in exclamation marks. It was good.

"Nicholas, that's brilliant. I'll buy it. Where the hell did it come from?"

He smiled shyly. "I don't know. I just don't like to do the obvious. So, you say something, and I take the opposite side. Then, I'm forced to follow another line of thinking and, somehow, I work out another level of understanding. I have to be pushed. You give good push."

That's how he likes to work. Always reaching. Always stretching into new possibilities. And when circumstances permit him to work that way, the physically damaging anguish he may be suffering from some other experience will actually recede and allow him to recover his health. He'll never forget his problem, of course. He obsesses far too much for that. But he will relax and enjoy some real moments of warmth and affection.

We usually worked from eight in the evening until one or two in the morning, when he didn't have to be on the set of *I Love Trouble* early. Sometimes his son Brawley,

who was with him at that time, would come in late after
playing with the gardener's two young daughters and hurl
himself at Nick. They'd wrestle on the couch for a few
moments before Brawley would curl against his father
and slowly fall asleep. The look of love on Nolte's face,
the tenderness of his embrace as he held his son, were
expressions of an emotion so deep, so pure and beautiful,
they would have melted the heart of the most cynical and
callous observer. I've seen Nick agonizing over minor dis-
turbances, tying himself and others so tightly in knots of
desperation that no one could get through to him, not
even Brawley. But these were times when he had no totally pleasant experience to balance him.

His preparation for *Jefferson in Paris* was totally pleasant.

As a result, his PVC vanished. He passed the film's
insurance examination easily, which eliminated another
serious element of stress. He'd been worrying constantly
about his heart's stopping with a stethoscope pressed
against his chest.

"Jesus, what'll happen if I have to pound myself to get
it going again? If I blackout while he's checking me? If I
don't pass? You think we ought to tell Merchant and Ivory
about this before it's too late for them to replace me? I
wouldn't want to put them in that kind of bind. I really
wouldn't. It's not fair to them."

"Tell them when they get here tomorrow. You'll feel
better, and they should know."

"Yeah, that's what I think."

Whatever shortcomings Nick may have, insensitivity
to what's right and wrong is not one of them.

His determination to be Thomas Jefferson knew no
bounds. Even to playing the violin. He knew, of course,
that the actual music would be dubbed in by a profes-

sional musician. Nevertheless, he practiced the specified music every day, and met with a teacher regularly, because he felt his fingering had to be absolutely correct for possible close-ups that would enhance the authenticity of the scene.

The violin lay on a table in the living room. In addition to his weekly lessons and his daily practice, he'd often pick it up just to run the melody a few times. It became a drug substitute, feeding his addiction to excellence. Needless to say, the sounds he made were always blasphemous. Even Beethoven, his beautiful, white Labrador, thought so. At the first note, the dog would flop on his side and whimper. Not howl or moan. Whimper. A cry for God's intervention. But Nick would persist, oblivious to the pain he was causing Beethoven and everyone else. And it paid off. Not only did his fingering improve steadily, his ease with the instrument—the way he lifted it, the way he held it—assumed a professional confidence that was consistent with the picture he was developing of Jefferson the musician.

No matter how hard he works, though, Nick Nolte is never certain that he sees his character. Certainty ends investigation. Believing he has his character would mean there's nothing more to do. But in his mind, there's always something else, so he must never believe he has him.

"Were getting him, Nick."

"Don't say that," he responded. "I don't see him. I don't know anything about him yet."

"What are you saying? We've talked about the way he stood, with his arms folded across his chest. And the way he sat when he was reading, practically on his spine, with his legs pulled up like a jackknife. You know the way he walked, with an easy, loose kind of step. You see all of that, don't you?"

"But that's nothing. I don't really know what the man looked like."

"You're crazy, we've got pictures of him all over the place."

"Yeah, and all of them are different."

A few days later, a series of events converged to help him. On a Saturday morning, at 10:30, two Academy Award-winning costume designers arrived from London to fit Nick with everything he was to wear in the film.

Nolte could hardly contain himself. He scooped up an outfit and hurried to another room. When he reappeared, the effect was amazing.

Jaws dropped. Eyes went wide.

"Oh, my," John Bright, one of the designers, murmured.

"Oh, yes," Jenny Beavan breathed.

Nick was euphoric. "Great! This feels great!"

He strode about, testing the feel of the garment before John and Jenny applied themselves to the necessary adjustments. He bent, stretched, twisted and sat. And when he lifted the violin and tucked it under his chin to measure the give of the waistcoat, everyone saw Thomas Jefferson in the room, even without a wig and makeup. Nick was delighted. Instead of complaining about costume discomfort, as most actors do, he welcomed every change: the back padding, the girdle, the off-balanced, high-heeled shoes. Everything.

Eric videotaped the entire fitting.

The next day, exactly at 11:00 A.M., a nose was carried carefully into the house. It came with two Italian prosthetics experts by way of Washington, D.C., where they had cast it from Houdon's famous bust of Jefferson.

After a perfect reproduction was applied to Nolte's face, he left the room and visited Eric, who was working at his computer, preparing notes for The Book. Their conversation turned on insignificant matters. Finally, eager to get back to his typing, Eric snapped, "What do you want? I don't understand. You need my help on something?"

Nick grinned. "You've already helped."

"What do you mean? What did I do?"

"Nothing. And that's what I was looking for."

"What's that supposed to mean?" Eric demanded.

"The nose. It works. If it had seemed unusual on my face, you'd have said something."

"Oh, my god—yeah, you have a Jefferson nose! It looks like it's yours, like it belongs on you! What a great job!"

An hour later, James Ivory and Ismail Merchant arrived. Nolte still wore the nose.

Examination and approval by the director and the producer comforted and encouraged him even more. He felt better about Jefferson. After they'd left, he beamed.

"I'm starting to see him," he said. "Just starting."

But he said that hesitatingly, as if the admission were something dangerous.

People who know Nick Nolte have said, "He saves his real feelings for his son and his work. When it comes to everyone else, he's friendly but there's no depth there."

True, but not entirely true.

In the quiet of a moment, when he's untroubled and gentle, he can express the sincerest warmth and affection in the most touching exchanges of the heart.

"Do you mind if I ask you a personal question?" he asked me one night.

"Not at all, Nicko. Go ahead."

The fire was blazing. The house was still. An air of calm and gentleness pervaded the room.

His words were soft. Interested. "How did you feel when Isabelle died?"

My wife had been killed in an automobile accident only three months earlier.

What followed was a long and memorable conversation about shock, about loss and love, about sorrow and recovery. I tried to describe the emotions her death had generated. And he told me about the death of his father, Frank, and what that had done to him. How it had devastated him, how he believed he'd never fully recovered from that loss, even to that day.

We talked long into the night. A wonderful discussion. No challenges. Nothing insistent. Just a beautiful heart-sharing exchange of our deepest thoughts and feelings. And when I finally stood to go back to the guest house, he stood also, and we embraced.

"Good night, my friend," he said softly in that gravelly voice. "This has been great. Thank you. Sleep well."

He may have been suffering arrhythmic trauma during those early days of his *Jefferson* work but, even though his heart wasn't functioning properly, Nolte had—and *still* has—a beautiful, tender heart inside that rugged body.

What gets in Nick's way, what prevents him from expressing this deeper significant part of himself easily to others, is his inability to translate what he learns from his work into everyday, interpersonal behavior. Understanding doesn't seem to change him. Despite having studied obsessive-compulsive behavior thoroughly, he's still obsessive and compulsive. Despite having examined anger carefully, he still erupts over trivialities. Despite having probed thoughtfulness deeply, he's still inconsiderate of others. And despite having explored the nature of love completely, he's still unable to sustain a warm and loving relationship with his women.

"You know what I need? I need a full, detailed description of love. Jefferson loved his wife dearly, enough to promise her on her deathbed that he'd never marry again. Then he falls madly in love with Maria Cosway. He's a very loving man. Incredibly restrained, like most other cultured people in the eighteenth century, but definitely loving. So what is love? How does it work? What's the nature and character of it? I need to know that."

To satisfy that need, a list of twenty-four characteristics of love was drawn from the screenplay, giving Nick the "handle" for his affair with Maria.

Some of them were:

1. Love is based upon choice and freedom
2. Love is beauty and, therefore, allows us to see and to appreciate beauty everywhere.
3. Love is pure, free of artifice.
4. Love is the source of happiness.
5. Love attracts; it never repels.
6. Love is sharing.
7. Love makes us attentive and caring.

He used the full list to sharpen his feelings for Maria Cosway. It enabled him to see her through genuine passion. But once the film was in the can, it was as if the ideas had never touched him—as though they had been solely an exercise of his acting art, with no relationship to the real world. He studies in order to learn more about life and himself, but what he learns does not have a lasting effect upon him.

One of his icons is J. Krishnamurti, who said, "I do not know what love is."

He will pronounce Krishnamurti's ideas with conviction, saying love can't exist when there's attachment, that the idea of life is to be free and detached, that only in detachment can love grow.

"The problem with women is they always have to hold on," he has said to me. "They don't know how to love without needing."

And in the matter of friendship, he's extremely wary.

"What's love got to do with it?" he asked suspiciously. "What does it mean?"

"Nothing terrible. Just being interested, caring, wanting to help, extending yourself for the benefit of the friend."

"I don't know," he said. "You have to be careful about that. It could lead to demands and expectations."

Of course, his kind of love isn't exactly what the women in his life have wanted or expected, nor does it generate warmth and closeness.

"I feel like he's always trying to stay out in front, all by himself," Vicki told me, "and he expects me to follow him and to try to catch up."

What has his concept done for him? Well, for one thing, it's created a rather solitary existence. True, he has many acquaintances in Hollywood. But that's all. By his own admission, no real friends. And for another thing, it's allowed him to delude himself terribly. To this day, Nolte believes his relationship with Vicki has been affected by a career that frightens her. His marriage to Sheila failed because her two children from a previous marriage made her unwilling to be with him wherever his acting would take him. And his marriage to Rebecca collapsed because she no longer had anyone to care for when he stopped drinking.

Consequently, if a woman loves Nolte, she has to love him on his terms, because he will not, and possibly cannot, adapt to her needs for any significant length of time. He says he's looking for freedom within love. Not the freedom of infidelity, because Nick is a monogamous man who still believes in marriage and would marry again, despite his three failures. But a freedom that, in his mind, exists in unconditional love, a total acceptance without judgment, a freedom from demands, requests and expectations, all of which, paradoxically, is something he seems to be incapable of offering to another living soul.

It's very interesting. Working as Thomas Jefferson, he understood love and had no trouble with it.

Living as Nick Nolte, he continues to flounder.

He's searching, though, always searching. Once, in a philosophical discussion, we touched upon spiritual rebirth. "I believe in a soul," he said, "but reincarnation? No. I can't go that far in my ideas about life. But I do believe we choose our way of dying. Why do you think we live? What's the reason?"

"Probably just to learn," I answered.

"To achieve nirvana?"

"I don't know about that. That portrays life as an ordeal, something to be escaped."

"It is an ordeal," he insisted.

"It can be tough, all right. But it's just experiences, painful and pleasant, all adding up to something beautiful."

He laughed. "I wish I could believe that, but I'm too fucked up to take that step."

In working with a gifted director, Nick must feel he's in harmony with his or her vision. He's not the kind of actor who wants to go off on his own and impose his interpretations on the film. Some actors believe the best director is the one who will leave them alone. Nolte believes the opposite: the best director is one who is thoroughly prepared and who, because of his or her understanding, is able to communicate ideas clearly in free and open discussion. In collaboration with such a director, Nick feels, the actor can do his best work and contribute significantly to the success of the project.

James Ivory is a director whose reputation precedes him. But Nolte had no idea how the man works. Naturally, he assumed a collaborative relationship. However, what he didn't know was that Ivory does not direct actors. Ivory leaves them alone. He is more interested in building the visual imagery of a scene than in guiding actors in their purposes and motivations.

"Except in the most extreme circumstances, I would never presume to tell an actor how to act," Ivory told me. "With any actor, even people who seem absolutely perfect for a part, it's still a kind of leap. They may not turn out to be all that perfect. You just have to do it, to trust that they'll be right."

After seeing Nolte in the Jefferson nose, after viewing

Eric's videotape of the costume fitting, and after reading some notes that would appear in The Book, Ivory offered, "I have a strange, wonderful feeling about the rightness of things. I may not be able to express the feeling clearly, but I know intuitively when something is wrong, and I have no feeling whatsoever that anything's wrong now."

Ivory said he agreed completely with the direction Nolte's preparation was taking him. He was impressed. He was excited. He was even filled with admiration. Easy things for him to say because his own understanding of Jefferson's personality and character was decidedly superficial compared to Nick's.

Now, this was not the kind of collaboration that Nick had hoped for; it left everything in his hands. But Ivory's approval was exactly what he needed then and, apparently, always needs. *Approbation. Stroking.* Nick must always hear positive things about his work or he gnashes his teeth and frets himself into depression. Approval from someone of Ivory's stature thrilled him; his approach to Jefferson was in harmony with the director's vision; they were on parallel tracks heading in the same direction. It made him look forward to the day he'd leave his personal problems behind and fly off eagerly to France. Meanwhile, buoyed by the director's high regard, he threw himself even more vigorously into his Jefferson investigations.

With the right encouragement, Nolte will destroy himself.

"I have to know what Jefferson sounded like. I can't just say the lines. Did he talk through his nose? Did he have a southern accent? Did he whisper?"

"Some descriptions say he had a high, thin voice, and

that's why he never liked to speak to crowds," I offered.

"I don't want to do that. I *can't* do that, not with my voice. Besides, I don't believe it. That's only speculation. I'd rather speculate in another direction."

"He may have a slight Scottish burr. He was strongly influenced by Scottish teachers."

"More speculation. The man was born here; he doesn't come from Scotland. America was a stronger influence than his teachers."

"Well, let's look at it this way, " I said. "He's southern aristocracy; until the Revolution, southern gentry identified with the British. So, give him a slight British accent, not too clipped, just enough precision to suggest the English influence and not enough to eliminate his American roots."

"That sounds reasonable. I'll need a tape of something like that so I can start to work on it. Damn! I wish I knew what he really sounded like. He was raised around slaves. Is there black speech in there? Did he have a southern accent? Did southern accents even exist back then? Damn!"

As fortune would have it, a few days later—

"Nick, I had to call you right away!"

"What's the matter? Anything wrong?"

"Hell, no! Everything's beautiful! You'll never guess what happened!"

"What?"

"I just heard an interview on PBS with a guy who's a language specialist. Not foreign languages, but—get this—*Jeffersonian southern dialect!* And he said he knew exactly how Jefferson and Washington spoke! He even imitated them!"

"Jesus, this is perfect! Just what we needed! Who is he?

How do we reach him?"

"His name's Hadley, Doctor Charles Hadley, and he teaches at Queen's College in Chapel Hill, North Carolina."

"Fantastic! I'll get Sherri on this immediately!"

Sherri did a superb job of locating Doctor Hadley. Messages left for him resulted in direct contact and willing participation in the elimination of Nolte's dilemma.

"Jefferson would have spoken as the Virginia elite," the doctor said. "His speech was not far from English speech, really, but it wasn't what we think of as the English of today. British English of today came into vogue in the middle of the eighteenth century. David Garrick, the actor, made it popular in London, and the Americans said no, no—we don't want that, and we pulled away and kept what was British speech from Warwickshire and Kent. And that's what has remained our southern speech. Jefferson's mother came from Warwickshire, and was quite an aristocratic person. So Jefferson would have adopted the speech of his mother."

"That's fascinating," Nolte said. "Then our southern speech today is really English speech and, until Garrick changed it, the English spoke with our southern accent."

"Exactly," Doctor Hadley agreed. Then he demonstrated Jefferson's speech, indicating it was not unlike contemporary Virginia rhythms and patterns. A very gentle and soft dialect with subtle, light inflections.

Nick grinned appreciatively. "I can do that. I can do that," he breathed.

Doctor Hadley offered to tape all of Nick's lines without interpretation, if a screenplay were sent to him.

Nick accepted gratefully.

A huge weight of concern had been lifted from his mind. But there would be other concerns—many oth-

ers—even if he had to invent them. If Nolte's not concerned about *some*thing in his quest for perfection, he's
not really happy.

"How'd you like to go to France?" he asked suddenly,
early in our work.

"What do you mean, spend a week there researching,
the way we did in Virginia and Washington?"

"No, I mean go to Paris for the shoot."

"The whole shoot?"

"Yeah."

"How long?"

"Thirteen weeks."

"That might be nice—yeah, I think I'd like that."

"Terrific. I'll pay the whole thing, okay? And there'll
be a per diem—y'know, so you have some spending
money while we're there."

"Sounds good. Could be expensive, though."

"How much could it cost—fifty, sixty thousand?"

"Easily."

"That's nothing. It'll be fun. We'll have a great time
together!"

"Okay, let's do it."

It's interesting. Years ago, when he was with Actors
Inner Circle, Nick used to beg dimes from everyone.

"Lemme a dime," he'd say, with his hand out and a
big, warm, irresistible grin on his face. "C'mon, will ya?
Lemme a dime. Don't be cheap."

It's impossible to estimate the number of dimes he
cadged with that approach.

"Why don't you carry your own money?" I'd chal-
lenge him. "You're not broke."

"I don't have pockets," he'd lie.

"*Bu-u-llshit!* You don't carry money because you *like* to bum dimes, and you like to bum dimes because you want to see if you can con people into giving them to you."

We'd be laughing.

"C'mon, gimme a dime," he'd persist. "Don't make it a big deal. Money means too much to you."

"I'm not going to give you a dime this time. You can't con me."

"You're controlled by money. That's your problem. You think money is important. It's not important. C'mon, don't be that way. Gimme a dime."

"You don't even know what money is," I countered once.

"I do so," he answered. "It's what made you a miser. Gimme a dime. Come on."

"It's what gives you freedom, you nut. Money allows you to make choices. And if you have enough of it for a lot of choices, you don't even think of it anymore."

"I'm free without it. And I can make choices. Right now, I choose to ask you for a dime. C'mon, gimme a dime, will ya? Make the choice to be generous and compassionate. Give this poor, humble actor a measly dime."

By now we'd both be laughing crazily. It was impossible to resist him.

"You win. Here's your dime."

And he'd take it as if he'd just won an enjoyable contest.

Which he had.

Today, he has enough money to spend over $50,000 without a moment's hesitation. Enough to satisfy every whim. Enough to take me to Paris with him for thirteen weeks, flying French Concorde, living at the Ritz Hotel, and enjoying everything first-class. Today, he doesn't bum dimes anymore because he carries thousands of dollars around with him, and he pulls out hundred dollar bills or credit cards to pay for anything that touches his fancy. Today, he has enough money for it to have little meaning to him. Perhaps, as Barbara Streisand told him, he's not rich. But that would be by Hollywood standards. By Nolte standards, where wealth only has relative value, Nick has sufficient money not to have to think about money anymore.

One dark night, while backing away quickly from the guest house, I accidentally rammed into the side of Vicki's new car. I was aghast at the extent of the damage I'd done. The entire passenger side had been caved in. Vicki was in New York at the time, winning acclaim for her reporter role in the Broadway show, *Damn Yankees*. I went to the main house to tell Nick of my carelessness.

"Jesus, I'm sorry. I didn't see her car there, and I was all screwed-up with this crazy idea that I had to take care of something immediately. It could have waited until tomorrow. I'm sorry, Nick. I'm really sorry."

"It's nothing," he said as we walked back to the guest house to assess the damage. "Don't be so upset."

"What's Vicki going to say?" I fretted.

"C'mon, will ya? It's nothing. It's only a car. Don't let it bother you."

We surveyed the wreckage.

"No problem," he said. "Vicki's not coming out for another five days. We'll have it fixed by then. It'll look like new."

"I'll pay for it," I offered.

"That's not necessary."

"Yes, it is," I insisted.

"Don't be ridiculous," he answered.

The next morning, Nolte had his secretary, Sherri, take care of the matter. The car was repaired quickly at a cost of thousands. It hadn't been covered by insurance. It had come out of his own pocket. And Nick never once mentioned the money he'd spent so freely on my blunder. He'd been not only generous, but wonderfully gracious about the entire incident.

To Nolte, money now has value only in respect to the solution of his immediate problems. If the problem is the cost of companionship in Paris, money solves it. If the problem is the repair of a car, money solves it. If the problem is a constant need to redesign and refurbish his house, money solves it. Money's there to be used, that's all, so he never concerns himself with how much something will cost. And his lack of interest is such that I seriously doubt he knows exactly how much he's worth without having to inquire for some specific and significant reason, like a divorce.

Around the time of the automobile accident, his relationship with Rebecca began to take a dangerous turn. He believed they had solved the financial problems of their separation amicably. He had drawn a list of all their assets on the blackboard of his study. Together, they'd worked out the terms. Cash was split down the middle. She received millions. Property was divided according to their individual needs. Since Rebecca wanted to get away from Hollywood, she took the house in Fort Lauderdale. Nick kept the place in Malibu. It was agreed that Brawley would remain with his mother and that Nick would have free access to his son. In the spirit of cooperation rather than contention, they even agreed upon a reasonable monthly figure for child support. Both had wanted the termination of their marriage to be as painless as possible for Brawley's sake. But they hadn't considered the influences of lawyers and acquaintances. Additional requests by Rebecca upset the equanimity they'd enjoyed in their own direct and very personal negotiations. It became a period of stress and unhappiness for both of them.

"I don't know what she wants," Nick complained. "We did it fairly, and now that doesn't seem to be enough. Her fucking friends are telling her to take all she can get. Every day she comes up with something new."

He'd identified his divorce simply as another problem that needed solving. Certainly a very large problem but, nevertheless, just another problem. And if money could solve it, then so be it. It wasn't the amount of cash involved that distressed him. It was his ingrained fear of being manipulated.

In Paris, Nolte would take his own per diem and throw it, actually toss it, onto a closet shelf. The long, wide shelf filled to overflowing with very large denominations of franc notes. How much was there never concerned him. It was there to be used. If a need arose, some problem of want, he'd stab his large hand into the mass of bills and grab a fist full of francs, stuff them into a pocket and start off for the Louvre in search of old-master prints, or for a walk through an art district in search of some other artifact for his Malibu home.

Today, Nick Nolte is far removed from his "Gimme a dime" days in Actors Inner Circle. However, though he can't deny the freedom that money has brought him, his indifference to its intrinsic value has remained the same.

Work on Jefferson continued at a regular, but increasingly intensive, pace. Nick began to put his lines down by taping them and practically living in his off-hours with a Walkman plugged into his ears. This practice of listening constantly to his speeches makes it easier for him to memorize the words when he actually directs himself to learning them verbatim. To Nolte, line memorization is extremely important. This comes from the early days of his theatrical training. Knowing his lines, having every word of them down pat, frees him from thinking about them. They become *his* words and, being his, he can grasp their emotional significance without constraint. He will have his entire script memorized perfectly before the first day of principal photography.

Discussions continued and more and more of Jefferson's character slipped into sharper focus. However, one last major point of investigation had to be considered in the Nolte process of acting preparation. That was the critical point of Key Concepts.

Key Concepts are the essential abstractions that thread themselves through the entire screenplay. Sometimes there is only one; sometimes there are as many as four or five. Identified, they become the central references for an understanding of everything that takes place in the script. In the case of *Jefferson in Paris*, there was a multiplicity of Key Concepts. And struggling with the Jefferson character, Nick labored endlessly to locate them. He knew that failure to identify them in the States would cause agonies in France. And agony there would affect not only his characterization but his working relationship with everyone on the set. Feelings of inadequacy cause Nick great pain, and when he's in pain, he knows he's impossible.

"Let's look at religion," he said to me one day. "Maybe there's something in that area."

"Okay, Jefferson was a deist. Many people called him an atheist, but they were wrong. He believed in God, but not in the way formal religions worshipped their gods. He had powerful religious convictions but no church affiliations."

"So we can say he had religious intensity."

"Wait a second, that's good. That could take us somewhere. He had powerful convictions and religious intensity—but they weren't attached to any church dogma. What *were* they attached to? To God alone?"

"No," Nick said. "To Jefferson, God was the Prime Mover but *Man* was responsible for his own condition on earth."

"That's good, Nick, that's good. Jefferson's religious convictions and his religious intensity should be attached to Man, not God. And that makes Man his religious *concern*, but what's his religion?"

"The cause of human freedom becomes his religion!"

"That's it! He devotes himself to the cause of human freedom as fervently as any priest or minister does to Christianity."

"And then he defines freedom," he continued. "To him, freedom is the right of choice. If we can make choices, we're free. Take that right away and we're enslaved."

"We're getting closer, Nick, I can feel it. So, if freedom is his religion, then anything obstructing or removing that right of choice—which he believes is mankind's by natural law—becomes a sin and tyranny over *Man's* mind."

"And that's why he writes: 'I have sworn upon the altar of God eternal hostility against every form of tyranny over the mind of Man.' Jesus, it fits!"

"And he believes two more things, Nick: one, that

Man means everybody, and two, that everybody has a conscience."

"And conscience means a sense of right and wrong, which becomes the basis of virtue and morality."

"What are we saying here? We're saying, freedom of choice allows Man to exercise his conscience. Right?"

"Right," he answered. "And with the free exercise of conscience, Man can then pursue the goals of life and happiness—"

"Two of our most important self-evident rights."

"That's it! That explains the Declaration of Independence!" he exploded.

"And his revolutionary passions!"

"And his hatred of monarchies!"

"And his belief in education!"

"And his commitment to America!" Nick exclaimed. "And his belief in people!"

"And his optimism!" I added.

"His interests! His actions! His feelings! Nick, his religion isn't Christianity—it's Freedom! The man was a religious zealot out to convert the world to Freedom!"

"That's it! Jesus, that's what I needed! It's the Key Concept!"

And for Nolte, it was. It was labeled "The Religious Zealot Key." However, it wasn't the only Key Concept. There would be four others, covering a total of five powerful personal forces working upon Thomas Jefferson. They came to be known as "The Covenant Key," which related to Jefferson's inviolable oath to his daughter, Patsy; "The Monticello Ideal Key," which identified Monticello as a microcosm of the American Dream, the place where Jeffersonian philosophy could be realized in actuality; "The Nature of Love Key," which clarified the differences between romance and reality; and "The Slavery Paradox Key," which addressed Jefferson's views on slavery.

Combined, the five concepts gave Nolte his precious keys to the final unlocking of the screenplay's secret doors. Thereafter, almost every Jefferson thought and action was measured by them, and a point was reached when Nick could say with some degree of satisfaction, "I'm starting to feel good about him now. I don't want to get complacent, because complacency stops the car, but I'm starting to feel good about him."

That day, identification of the Key Concepts produced a sense of euphoria that led Nolte to suggest, "We ought to write this someday."

"Write what?"

"This whole thing. How we go about it. The Process. It might help other actors."

"It might. If they're willing to work this hard."

"Do you think anybody else works like this?"

"I don't know if everybody works exactly this way, but if he's a good actor, he prepares."

"You think so?"

"What's wrong? You seem troubled all of a sudden."

"Oh, I heard Anthony Hopkins say he doesn't prepare for a role, that he just reads the script and goes in and does it."

"And that bothers you?"

"Fuck, yes! I work like hell, and he just goes in and does it? That makes me feel like nothing."

"Well, pull yourself together, Nicko, because it's probably garbage. Nobody gets the kind of sensitive understanding that Hopkins expresses without preparation. Statements he makes are all part of the business. You know that. Media consumption. Have enough interviews and you have to come up with all kinds of nonsense. He prepares. Believe me."

Nolte was relieved. He hates to believe he's inferior to anyone in any aspect of his acting talent. He laughed. "I'm getting too old for this."

He was fifty-three, then.

"How many years do you think I have left?" he asked.

"You'll probably die from PVC tomorrow."

"No, seriously. How many years do you think I have left as an actor?"

"Well, if you take good care of yourself physically, and you choose the right roles, you could last another fifteen years."

"You think so? That much? I'd say, the most, ten."

"You're probably right. Fifteen would be the outside limit, and that's only if you take good care and get good scripts. What'll you do when it's over?"

"I don't know."

"Direct?"

"Naahhh."

"Produce?"

"I'm no producer. I'm an actor. That's all I can do."

"There's always Broadway. That's something you've never done."

"Doing a play is too hard. All those lines to remember."

Actually, the theater is where Nolte really belongs. As strong as his work is in films, it pales against what used to be his power on the stage. There, he was an awe-inspiring presence. He commanded attention, and the depths of his sensitivity evoked audience reactions that are remembered to this day. Unfortunately, despite the hard work he puts into each of his films, motion pictures have made him soft and fearful.

Film-making is safe for the actor. There are always unlimited takes and the comfort of editing to protect him. He knows that his performance on the screen isn't true, that he never did it, that it's only the product of dislocated snippets of acting, the best of his moments put together by someone else in a cutting room. And he can feel safe in that knowledge. But acting on the stage is another matter. There, he's exposed, in the flesh, not on celluloid, for two hours, not a few minutes at a time, and he's horribly vulnerable. There, he has only one chance in each performance to get it right. And if he fails, he's wounded terribly. "What happens if I forget my lines? What happens if I suddenly blank-out and lose it? I'll die!" he worries, because he knows that dying onstage is a terrible, terrible death.

Nolte won't admit that fear readily now, but it's there, and it scares him enough to make him unwilling to return to the dangerous theater where he began his acting career.

"No Broadway," he insisted. "When my days in film are over, I'll just walk away."

"And become a nice, fat vegetable."

"It'll be restful and beautiful," he said with a laugh. But his laughter had a note of regret and apprehension in it. "Rod Steiger told me to take everything they offer," he added quietly, "because someday they won't be offering anything."

"He hurts?"

"Badly."

"Well, I don't think you have to worry about that right now, but what you'll do with your life down the road is something that deserves some consideration."

"I guess so."

Nolte tries to appear indifferent to the Orange Principle of motion picture production, that practice of squeezing the box-office juice from a talent and then callously throwing away the crushed rind. However, he is concerned. He knows the days of all actors are numbered, and that his number is coming up. He tries to deny his concern with statements about the beauty of retirement, about his need for rest, but little comments like "I'm thinking of having a little face work done" and "I'd really like to work with Terry Gilliam" belie his bravado.

Despite creeping anxieties about the inevitable end of his acting career, though, Nick has retained his wonderful sense of humor. He's a great storyteller. His tales are almost always about his location experiences, wild things that have occurred during the making of a film. And he tells his stories with gusto, often punctuating colorful descriptions with infectious bursts of laughter that have his listeners roaring.

"One day, while I was eating, one of my caps came off. I didn't realize it right away, so I wound up swallowing it. Well, I had to get that cap back, and I figured it would take a while, so I didn't shit for two days. They had me in a fancy hotel where I could get good room service. So, after breakfast in my room, I took the morning newspaper and my knife and fork and went into the bathroom. I mean, this place was classy. Beautiful toilet. But I spread the newspaper on the floor and squatted. I didn't want to lose that cap in the toilet bowl. Well, after two days of holding it in, I shit a turd big enough to fill the bath tub. And somewhere in that turd was my cap. What could I do? I dug in with my knife and fork. I worked on that thing for an hour. I dug out pieces of corn, pieces of potato, pieces of carrots, but I couldn't find the damn cap. I had to give up. There I was with a mashed turd all over this newspaper. I couldn't flush everything down the toilet. It was too big. I didn't know what the hell to do with it. So I folded it up and put it on the breakfast table. But then I figured room service might think it was pretty strange when they collected the dishes. So I went into the hall and tried to put it on somebody else's breakfast cart. But people came out of their room then, and they saw me just as I was about to drop it on their tray, so I took it back to my room. There was a little balcony, so I opened the door and went out to get rid of this thing. I was going to toss it on the lawn, and let somebody try to figure where the hell it came from, but I was right over the pool and there were guests already swimming. What could I do with it, huh? I got dressed. I thought I'd dump it in a garbage can on the street. But when I got in the elevator, I wasn't alone. Some people recognized me, and they wanted my autograph. I couldn't say no. So, I asked them to hold this thing while I signed their papers. They had some very strange expressions as the smell filled the elevator. And they couldn't wait to give it back to me and get the hell out of there when the doors opened. Everywhere I went, I was walking in a vapor of shit. And I couldn't find a garbage can. Finally, I did the only thing I could. I hailed a cab, took a short ride, and left the damned thing there for the next customer. And I never did get that cap."

Nolte's never afraid to tell a story about himself that makes him look ridiculous. It's part of his confidence. He knows he's in control of the moment, and self-disparagement is an engaging form of humility.

"Has Nick told you about his Borneo experience yet?"

Eric asked with a cryptic smile on his face.

"No, what's the Borneo story?"

"Have him tell you."

When I asked about it, Nolte responded immediately with his customary enthusiasm, telling it with dramatic movements, and in colorful detail. It's one of his favorite exploits, having happened to him during the Borneo filming of *Farewell to the King*. It's a story of jungle treks, and fierce natives, and tribal induction rites, and animal sacrifice, and a wild, aboriginal feast. It's not one of his humorous stories. Instead, it's one of high adventure, a lengthy tale, with moments of enthralling suspense, in an exotic setting.

"Did he tell you about going through the jungle?" Eric asked me later.

"That was quite a hike."

"We were in a jeep."

"What about the natives? They sounded wild."

"They were wearing Nike sneakers and T-shirts."

"You're kidding!"

"The story gets a little better every time he tells it."

"What about the induction rites? Didn't that happen?"

"That happened. They got into costume, smeared some paint on his face and gave him a spear."

"And then he killed that pig for the sacrifice. Eric, whatever you say, that took some guts. I couldn't have done it."

"He couldn't either. They had to come up behind him, hold the spear, and kinda force him to do it."

"But that feast must have been sensational."

"Yeah, that was great. We all got into the jeeps and went to a Chinese restaurant."

Nolte enjoys telling his stories so much, he has a tendency to elaborate on details until the incidents are considerably distorted from the actual experience.

Departure day for Paris was approaching quickly. A new problem had developed: where was Eric going to reside while we were in France?

Always the producer, Ismail Merchant believed he could cut costs by placing Eric in a cheaper hotel near the Ritz.

"No way!" Nolte snapped. "You and me in one hotel and Eric in another? No way!"

"How'll you handle it?"

"Tell him, that's all. Eric has to be with us. I need him close. We'll be working right up to the final wrap. I can't have Eric running over every time there's something for him to do just so Ismail can save a few bucks. Let him find the money someplace. Eric stays with us or I don't go!"

Staying in another hotel was not a bad idea as far as Eric was concerned. Proximity to Nolte during the shooting of a film is usually so harrowing for him that he welcomes any opportunity not to be in his company. But Nick would have none of that.

"We stay together," he fumed. "I'm gonna need the both of you every minute we're there."

As Nolte's assistant, Eric was on the film's payroll, and where he'd stay was entirely up to Ismail Merchant. Ismail is a man who hates to be thwarted. He's an extremely congenial man, a man who assumes an engaging, fatherly posture with everyone in the production. He's also generous and considerate of other people's feelings. But when it comes to his position as producer, he can go absolutely berserk when he's challenged.

One day, I entered the *Jefferson in Paris* production office just as the following exchange was taking place between Ismail and a group of production personnel that included the production manager, Humbert Balsan, and Frederic Nicolas, the second unit's first assistant director:

ISMAIL
What the fuck is going on?!

HUMBERT
We're trying to organize—

ISMAIL
Well, why the fuck isn't it organized?!

FREDERIC
I've been—

ISMAIL
I've never seen anything like it!! This fucking production has more fucking directors—!!

HUMBERT
So what do you want to do?

ISMAIL
I'm not going to pay for cranes and people who just stand around waiting!!

HUMBERT
Fine. Then cancel the shot. Get rid of the equipment, get rid of the—

ISMAIL
Every fucking thing goes wrong because nobody knows what the fuck he's doing!!

FREDERIC
I'm working twenty-hour days—

ISMAIL
We're all working twenty-fucking-hour days!!!!

FREDERIC
I asked—

ISMAIL
Ask me! Ask *me!* I'm the fucking boss here!!!!

This is the tight-fisted producer Nick was now challenging, but what Ismail Merchant didn't know at the time
was that Nick Nolte is a man who can go as berserk as he
when his own critical demands are being questioned or
opposed. The difference between them is that Ismail
enjoys facing a problem like this directly, while Nolte,
preferring to remove himself from face-to-face confrontation, will have his agent and lawyer handle the matter.

"What do you mean, you won't go?" I asked Nick.
"You have a contract."

"Not yet."

"Not yet? You mean, they've gone through all the cos-
tuming, all the preparations for you, and they don't have
you signed to a contract? What, are they crazy?"

"That happens a lot. I've started pictures before while
they're still working out contract particulars."

This time, no contract worked to Nolte's advantage.

Ismail was in Paris at the time, so he was at a decided
*dis*advantage in this skirmish. He couldn't meet with
Nolte to exercise his considerable charm over him. He
could only fume in France.

The intercontinental telephone calls raged, and Nick
held his ground.

Finally, realizing that Nolte was truly adamant about
this, Ismail Merchant relented. There was nothing else he
could do. It was either that or lose his star only days away

from the start of filming. Eric would be housed at the Ritz Hotel with Nick and me, on the same floor, in an adjoining room. We will never know what, if any, kind of profanity gushed from Ismail Merchant's mouth at this crimp in his budget and bruise to his authoritarian ego. He's much too clever and suave to express a sense of defeat. All of his future contacts with Nolte were dressed in smiles and pleasantries, as if he were delighted that Nick had been satisfied.

And, true to form, Nolte basked in the warmth of his victory. The motion picture industry is a battleground to him, filled with people who are interested only in furthering their own ends—people who, like himself, detest frustrations and inconveniences in the realization of their own goals. This time, he had won; it was a good feeling.

He was ready for the final step in his preparation. He had The Book, which was constantly growing. He had his Key Concepts. Now, he would have to identify his Emotional Arcs. To Nolte, every screenplay has an emotional arc, a sweep of feelings, first within each scene, and then from scene to scene throughout the script. Working with character, lines and action will lead him to the identification of individual emotions; then, collectively, these emotions form a flow, an arc of feelings. With his emotional arc clearly defined, he has a firm grasp of the scene and, ultimately, of the entire film.

"All right, so in this scene, Jefferson's going with Lafayette to one of Mesmer's seances. He's going because he's been told that his broken wrist may be healed there. There's a little bit of hope in him. But at the same time, he doesn't really believe in hypnotism. He's skeptical, even a little resistant. Then, when he sees the nonsense that goes on there, he jumps up and runs out. He's disgusted. Outside, he tells Lafayette strongly he won't have anything to do with charlatans. He's flat-out angry. So I go from a little hope with some resistance to disgust to anger. That's my emotional arc for the scene."

With that understanding, Nolte moves on. He never tries the scene. He never expresses the emotions. He believes he will lose the realism of spontaneity if he does. That has to wait for his moment before the camera.

"Okay, Nick, you have three emotional possibilities for this moment when Jefferson learns of the death of his little girl back in Virginia. Right?"

"Right."

"Which one will you use?"

"How should I know? I can't decide that now. It'll be one of them, but which one? Who knows? It'll just happen. I can't shape it. That wouldn't be real or honest."

Before going on a set for a scene, Nick will go over his lines repeatedly and refresh his memory about the scene's emotional arc. Then he trusts to that understanding and relaxes into the moment. He never tries to become the character. He is always himself within his clear understanding of the character's manner, speech and thought. Trying to be the character is performance, and performance is acting, he believes. Actors are never supposed to act. They're supposed to *be*. In *being*, there is reality.

The day finally arrived. After seven months, he was eager to get to France. Tired, but eager. He would still have work to do on *I Love Trouble*. Three days of dubbing, by his contract. But that would have to be done in a Paris studio with a long distance hook-up to Los Angeles.

"I'm going to enjoy this shoot," he said enthusiastically. "Y'know, a good experience can wipe away the taste of a bad one."

"Agreed. You'll forget about *I Love Trouble* and Julia Roberts soon enough."

"I think so. James Ivory seems all right. I like him."

"And Ismail Merchant?"

"He's all right, too."

Of course, his reactions would have been different if he'd lost his little battle with Ismail. And if Ivory, for whatever reason, were in his artistic way. The absence of resistance is a sublime state of affairs for Nick.

But a few days later, and five days before we were to leave for France, he waved a fax at me.

"I just got new lines from Ivory."

No doubt about it, he was agitated.

"What's the problem?" I asked.

"They've added something that turns Jefferson into a hypocrite and a fraud."

"How?"

"Here, look at it!"

In trying to put a twentieth century racial spin on the Declaration of Independence, the new line had Jefferson admitting that the document is dishonest because what he really meant was: all *white* men are created equal, not *all* men.

To Nolte, this nullified the basic tenet of the entire manuscript, and weakened Jefferson's character immeasurably. The line created all kinds of problems for him. But most of all, it made him start to wonder about James Ivory's grasp of his own screenplay.

"How could he *do* this?" he fretted. "Doesn't he understand Jefferson?"

"Maybe not. Maybe the whole thing's going to be in

your hands."

"Well, I can't say this line! What am I gonna do? We have to get him to drop it!"

In the blink of an eye, fretting can become obsession.

"Take it easy. We'll get a letter off to him, explaining your objections, and it'll all be worked out."

James Ivory is a very open man. He recognizes his mistakes readily and, without defensiveness, makes the necessary adjustments. The problem was solved quickly and congenially.

Nick was happy again. But the incident alerted him to the possibility of subsequent errors and, though he responded positively to Ivory's direction, he never quite trusted the man after that. And that's pure Nolte. He expects his directors to be gifted in all areas of their craft—people who offer knowledge, understanding and skill. And when a director exhibits weakness in any of these areas, Nick feels the creative ground under him begin to shake.

No matter how well prepared he may be himself, no matter how clearly he sees his character and what that character must do, he expects and needs the strength of a proficient director who doesn't make blatant mistakes, even if that director may never say a word to him on the set.

We were ready to leave. Eric had done a masterful job of packing. Boxes and boxes of Jefferson books, notes, and assorted materials—tape recorders, tapes, batteries, lap top computers, cellular telephones, paper, pens, pencils—everything, even down to paper clips and rubber bands. There would be no shortage of our work essentials in Paris.

Nick threw a load of clothes onto a living room table. He can't stand restrictive apparel; so, much of the gear was his well-known, floppy-loose hospital garments and other nondescript things, like an almost-ankle-length, black cashmere coat, some heavy slipover shirts and long, oversized sweaters. Nolte abhors formality. At that time, I believe, despite the social functions he was occasionally forced to attend, he didn't even own a tuxedo. And if he *did* own one, he loathed the idea of wearing it, even as he does today. The clothes on that table would have to suffice for his entire thirteen weeks in Paris.

He was ready. Or thought he was.

When he was expected to pack his own boxes, he almost had a stroke.

"I don't know how to do that," he pleaded comically. "Eric, get all that stuff in the boxes for me, will you?"

His wheedling didn't work. Eric refused. I refused. And in the end, he had to do it himself. The use of his time in mundane activity, even when that activity is related to an immediate need, is anathema to Nolte. He's so used to having other people relieve him of that responsibility that he truly believes himself to be above it. Of course, he does many things for himself, like driving and, occasionally, cooking, but when it comes to the trivial things of living, he rather expects other people do them for him.

The plan was to go to New York for two days before taking the Concorde to Paris. Vicki was waiting for Nick there. Their affair had become especially hot in the past seven months, with Vicki flying to Los Angeles to spend time with Nick whenever she could, and with daily tele-

phone calls that lasted for hours, at any time of the day
or night. *Damn Yankees* was playing at the Marriott
Marquis Theater; it was decided, for convenience sake,
that we would stay in the Marriott Hotel. Nolte wasn't
exactly happy about this. Wherever he goes, he prefers to
stay in suites, in the best hotels the area has to offer. In his
mind, the Marriott, though conveniently located and sat-
isfactorily operated, didn't offer the soothing elegance
and sense of privacy to which he's become accustomed.
And this is an interesting paradox in the man. On the one
hand, he disdains the trappings and the style of wealth
while, on the other, he enjoys settling anonymously into
them with a kind of comfortable sense of belonging. He's
something like a down-home boy who likes to lose himself in quiet luxury.

Around this time, the feud between Disney's CEO,
Michael Eisner, and Chairman of Walt Disney Studios
Jeffery Katzenberg was coming to a head. This was
important to Nolte, because Disney was financing, and
would be distributing, *Jefferson in Paris*, and Katzenberg
had been responsible for green-lighting the entire project.
Eisner was refusing to give Katzenberg the promotion he
demanded, and Katzenberg was threatening to leave the
studio if he didn't get his way. No one knew what the outcome of the battle would be. But the night Nolte attend-
ed a performance of *Damn Yankees* to watch Vicki in
action, a somewhat tired-looking man walked up the aisle
during intermission, smiled interestingly at Nick and said
a few words of greeting as he went past.

"Who was that?" I asked.

"Joe Roth."

"Big man."

"If Katzenberg leaves Disney, I think Roth may take

his place."

"So?"

"It'll affect the film."

"How?"

"I don't know, but it'll be in a big way."

Sadly, six months later, Disney infighting would justify this nebulous fear.

Nick's years in the motion picture business have given him a special sensitivity to the dangers of change. He likes to see himself as a daring figure, a maverick, someone who's unaffected by the vagaries of the industry. He likes to believe his understanding of the industry's machinery has immunized him to all the strains of fear it has created. And, in a sense, he's right. He *does* understand how the business works. Very clearly and in great detail. But immunization against anxiety in film-making is a dream, and Nolte is still as susceptible to the disease as he ever was. Though Joe Roth's quiet greeting that night in the Marquis Theater didn't bring Nolte down with a case of jitters, it did alert him to the possibility of damage to his work in the Jefferson role.

After the performance, we went backstage to see Vicki. The warmth, the tentative touch and kiss with which they greeted each other indicated to anyone watching that theirs was a beautiful, budding romance. Vicki was charmingly nervous; Nick was unusually shy. It was lovely.

Of course, everyone recognized him, and though Nolte was the outsider, the power of film celebrity is such that, even though he was among fellow performers, he was greeted with that special deference usually associated with royalty. The eager, but subdued, smiles. The gentle handshakes. The quiet comments. The tentative questions. The self-conscious laughter. Very few people treated him with the camaraderie of equals.

And how does Nolte react to those circumstances? With quiet, friendly enthusiasm, as if he feels like a non-member, someone who wants to belong, who wishes to be accepted as a peer.

Only one person satisfied that desire. He was not a member of the cast. He was another film celebrity, who, like Nolte, was visiting backstage. He was Martin Short.

And when he and Nolte greeted each other—! The pleasure! The laughter! The shouting! It was as if they were long-separated, old, old friends. In actuality, they had rarely, if ever, socialized together. They never telephoned each other. They almost never saw each other. In short, they didn't really know each other. But here they were, gushing like long-lost brothers, only because they had once done a picture together, and because both were now out of place and ill at ease in the backstage setting of *Damn Yankees*.

Vicki watched this quietly and, I believe, she understood: stardom has not put Nolte at ease with himself outside his movieland environment; on the contrary, it has made him more withdrawn, and comfortable only with other members of the Hollywood Tribe.

No work was done during the two days we were in New York. Eric and I didn't even see Nolte. But Vicki did, every moment she was available.

"You've really got it for this one," I commented on our way to JFK to board the Concorde for Paris.

He grinned happily. "Yeah," was all he answered, but

the way he said the word showed how deeply he was falling in love.

"Good for both of you. Maybe she's the one, Nick. Four could be your lucky number."

"Maybe," he said.

Vicki Lewis is a lot of woman. Exceptionally intelligent. Fast-witted. Vibrantly alive. Excited and exciting. Incredibly talented. And hungry for a lasting love. She isn't the kind of woman to accept a subservient or subordinate role to any man. With Vicki, their love would have to be based on equality. And I'm sure Nick had some tremors of uncertainty about that even as he released himself to the beauties of this new relationship.

The entire seven months in the States had been filled with a kind of joyous communion. We'd worked very hard. We'd shared thoughts, insights, personal experiences. We'd dined together, walked together and laughed together. In all that time, there had never been a cross word between us, never a harsh sound. The best of Nick Nolte had been his only face.

But Nolte has a few other faces—some of them quite ugly—and all of them would be worn in Paris.

Four

The Concorde left JFK at 1:00 P.M. on the third day in April; it landed at Charles De Gaulle Airport outside Paris three hours and eighteen minutes later. It had traveled an average 1500 MPH at an altitude around 59,000 feet, smoothly and quietly. Nick would have enjoyed the extraordinary attendant service, and the trace of planet curvature below, if he hadn't been napping almost all the way over the Atlantic Ocean or listening to Doctor Hadley's tape of his lines in Jefferson's voice. He had glanced through the window casually, satisfied his interest and quickly accepted the experience. It was as if he were beyond excitement, as if he had become jaded about everything in which he was not personally and intimately involved. His focus from here on would be entirely on Thomas Jefferson. There would be moments of interest in other things of course and pleasure, but only moments, and they would be simply of interest and pleasure, never of pure excitement.

The Concorde floated to earth; we deplaned into cold, windy, rainy weather. Ismail Merchant and Humbert Balsan were waiting. They welcomed Nolte warmly and escorted him through customs where, because of the producer's influence, passports were stamped routinely but expeditiously. The drive to the Ritz Hotel was marked by Ismail's enthusiastic descriptions of the accommodations and by his promises of an exceptionally enjoyable filming experience.

Like an aristocrat being told that his rarefied requirements were assured satisfaction, Nolte was pleased. And when he saw the three rooms that were to be ours for the next three months, he was even happy.

Nick's "room" was a suite, a small suite to be sure because of Ismail's penurious budgetary considerations, but one large enough to afford Nolte the sense of space he's come so implacably to believe he needs.

My room was a fairly large room adjoining Nick's, and Eric's was a small, almost closet-like space adjacent to mine. The thick, padded doors connecting all three were kept open during most of the day, allowing the kind of free access that prompted Eric with clear derision to name our accommodations something like Camp Wongatonga. But that didn't come for a week or so. Though it would soon change, the first few days after our arrival were charged with enthusiasm. Nick was to go before the cameras in a week, and all three of us prepared eagerly for that day.

We had landed in France at 11:00 P.M. By twelve, we were in our rooms. By 1:00 A.M., Nolte was ready for something, anything. His body was on New York time— 5:00 P.M. Rested from his transatlantic napping, he said he needed one of his walks.

"Now?" I objected. "The city's locked-up, and it's raining."

"It's only drizzling. C'mon, let's see what's out there. Don't be a drag. We're in Paris, f'r Chrissake. Ten minutes, that's all."

"Ten minutes?"

"No more."

"Okay, let's go."

Those ten minutes became an hour and a half. Not because we wanted that to happen. But because all three of us became so thoroughly lost after two wrong turns that we were unable to find our way back to the hotel even with the help of a Parisian couple, who were also trying to escape the rain.

"What did they say?" Nick asked.

"They said we go down two blocks, traverse a street toward the Napoleon column, then cut right, and we'll be three blocks from the Canadian border. How the hell should I know what they said?" I sputtered. "I don't speak French!"

Drenched, we laughed hysterically through the entire experience.

At one point, searching desperately, we couldn't find a place where Nolte could buy a pack of cigarettes, and he was close to having a nicotine fit. But even that didn't dampen his delight in our situation.

"I want my bath and dry clothes!" I shouted, standing in the middle of a dark and empty street.

"I want my cigarettes!" Nick bellowed, joining me.

"I want my mommy!" Eric wailed.

And we all collapsed in a laughing heap, in the middle of the gutter.

That's another interesting characteristic about Nolte. He can tolerate extreme discomfort when it's connected to a ludicrous situation. But the slightest inconvenience under normal circumstances will throw him into a frenzy. He'll often justify his distress with a rationalization about the demands of his work—how disturbance prevents him from concentrating on a scene and its problems—but the fact is he's an extremely volatile man. He's a fuse, always waiting to be ignited. Of course this becomes infinitely disconcerting to those who work with him. They treat him then with apprehension and caution. And when the fuse is sizzling, they either run away and leave him to himself, or they stand by impotently, waiting for it to fizzle out. In a real sense, Nolte is a man of shifting moods and emotional extremes—someone, however, who is struggling constantly and unsuccessfully for lasting self-control.

Through another accidental but lucky turn, we located a street that looked faintly familiar, and we finally found our way back to the hotel. The way we charged into the lobby, laughing raucously with relief, probably made the night clerk think his three new American guests were gloriously drunk. But that would be nothing compared to what some of the Ritz's personnel would think of us after thirteen weeks. I'm sure by then they believed we were unquestionably insane.

Like millions of other Americans, Nick is an insomniac. A full night's sleep is elusive even in the best of times. And when he's working, the stress he feels makes it impossible for him to sleep at all without the help of pills. Since he can't bear tossing ceaselessly throughout the night, and he must feel rested for the next day's shoot, he's resorted to their use so frequently that he's become sleeping-pill dependent, which of course is a euphemistic way of saying he's addicted to them. That rainy night in Paris, for whatever reason, he collapsed exhaustedly on his bed. And for the first time in five years, he slept four straight hours without the help of a single pill. A truly remarkable accomplishment, inasmuch as he usually takes at least three of his knockout bombs at a time.

Nolte on location is a different man from Nolte in Malibu. Especially when he's the star of a production. Something very strange and interesting happens. It's as if he has a hidden persona, someone just under the surface of his actions, waiting to be released by a corrupting force of involvement.

"I get crazy," he warned, "and it gets worse the deeper we get into production. You'll see."

This suggests he has no control over his Mister Hyde. That the demon surfaces because of inevitable circumstances. In a way, he's right; Hyde does appear without being summoned. However, his ugly face isn't revealed suddenly. It peeks out in little comments, at first. In small acts of impatience. These grow slowly into biting remarks. And unreasonable demands. In time, Nolte stops requesting. He orders. There must be no resistance to the satisfaction of his needs. Resistance drives him either wild or into a funk. As time passes, almost all traces of consideration disappear. Annoyance and, sometimes, even contempt take their place. He becomes totally self-absorbed and unappreciative. This should make him obnoxious to everyone. But it doesn't. Why? Because his saving grace is his fear of being disliked. Failure to be liked confuses and disorients Nick. And though he says he's beyond caring, he tries to avoid unpleasantness at all costs. Consequently, he's charming to everyone in the production. He's bright, winningly congenial and extremely funny whenever he's not isolating himself in his dressing room. He reserves Mister Hyde for his assistant. For this reason, Eric, who's done almost a dozen films as Nick's amazingly conscientious and supremely efficient aide, finds proximity to him during any shoot a harrowing experience. Nick's assistant must be his whipping boy, there to solve all problems that will disturb him, always ready to eliminate anything that will intrude upon his energies. And if something should not go exactly right, there to take his abuse.

Nick recognizes when he's being objectionable, but he makes no effort to check himself. What he doesn't recognize is why he's so offensive. In production, Nolte feels he's part of a select coterie of people, all arranged in concentric circles of importance. The few tight, inner circles are the Core Groups—producers, director, fellow actors, everyone in the above-the-line category of budgetary parlance; the other circles hold the below-the-line personnel, all the way to the outer rim of lowly production assistants. Now, every one of these people bears directly upon Nick's daily work before the cameras. In one way or another, they're all involved in the actual, physical shooting of the film.

Strange as it may seem, his own personal assistant doesn't fit into that reference. Even though he may be on the production payroll, Nick's assistant belongs to *him*, not to the hands-on filming of the story. In that position, then, he doesn't merit the same consideration that Nolte will express in varying degrees to everyone else. Furthermore, if the assistant happens to be his nephew, someone whose affection he's sure of, then with no fear of being disliked to hinder him, Nick shows no restraint whatsoever in his moodiness with him. He feels totally free to rant at him whenever he's upset or to enjoy the relationship in his off-hours with all kinds of wild and crazy behavior. A compliant helper who understands and at the same time cares for him is the perfect foil for Nick Nolte's location madness. And with me in Paris as well, believing he had *two* foils, Nolte felt his cup had surely *runneth over.*

In the earliest days of our arrival Nick was still totally agreeable and surprisingly playful. Now, however, his amusement took the form of obscene physical attacks. In the privacy of our rooms, he'd suddenly grab Eric from behind, hold him, and simulate sexual movements. He knew the effect this would have on him. It infuriated Eric. And when Eric responded with wild efforts to break loose and imaginative threats like, "I'll rip off your scrotum and jam it down your throat!" or "I'll hit you so hard your ancestors will feel it!" Nick was delighted.

Until he became deeply involved in the filming schedule, hardly a day went by when Nolte didn't inflict some kind of playful torment upon Eric. Sometimes, it was by invading his room and rubbing his bare bottom on his bedsheet with comments about having run out of toilet paper; sometimes it was by holding him in a death grip and trying to kiss him with exaggerated pleas about familial affection. But whatever the act was, it always drove Eric wild. And every time it worked, it brought Nolte great pleasure.

"Did you see him?" Nick asked. "He went crazy."

"And you like that."

"Yeah."

"Why?"

"He's too uptight. I'm just tryin' to loosen him up. He knows I'm only kidding."

In time, unable to stop Nick with a direct approach, Eric convinced him to mount attacks on me. Together, they would storm my room, and a three-way wrestling match would ensue in which shouts and laughter were loud enough to have been heard in Australia.

These mad outbursts took place even in the hotel's tiny elevator and usually had us tangled in a squirming mass on the floor until the doors were about to open. Then we'd arrange ourselves quickly and exit in the most dignified way. What we didn't know at the time was that a hotel security camera was capturing every second of our insane behavior and that somewhere in the vaults of the Ritz Hotel there would be enough raw material to please the rapacious appetites of a dozen tabloid editors.

While he feels free in his speech and actions at almost all times, Nick won't behave in this maniacal fashion with everyone. Only with those who will join him and with whom he feels close enough not to be judged harshly.

The boxes arrived. We spent the morning unpacking, after which all three of us collapsed. Jet lag—it would dog us for days. Despite his physical exhaustion and the trials of an adjustment period, though, Nolte still felt driven to do *some*thing related to his role, even if it was only a read-through of the screenplay. Not a day will go by, on *any* film, when this will not be true. He's conscientious about this to the point of being compulsive.

Reading with Nolte requires conformity to a kind of remote informality. He needs someplace to recline, he can't wear shoes, and his clothing must be extremely loose. He believes he thinks best unencumbered and on his back. In addition to this, whoever is with him must be at an appreciable distance. He thinks nearness of another body is an invasion of his intellectual space, and then he's not free to explore the deeper possibilities of his thoughts. Actor madness? It certainly is. Why? Because Nolte thinks very well with his shoes on, standing on his feet and in passionate, nose-to-nose confrontation.

"You sit over there. The couch is mine."

"Okay, I'll just pull this a little closer."

"No! No! I can't think if you're too close."

"Too close? I'm practically in the next room."

"No, that's good, that's good. You don't have to be in my lap, do you? Let's read."

Also, in his waking hours he continued his long walks.

Rain, wind, clouds, biting cold—nothing could deter him. Long walks are an essential part of his life. And he always likes company. Why he needs someone to accompany him is a mystery, because most often he prefers to walk by himself, sometimes even crossing the street to be far away from his companion. With his hands clasped behind his back, shoulders hunched, he ambles along, stopping occasionally to study a display in a window or to enter a store for silent browsing, all the while listening to his lines on a Walkman tape recorder. Being with Nick on one of his walks can give one the feeling of being an addendum. It's as if you're with him, but he's never with you, as if he expects you to trail after him and to be there when and if he should decide to share a thought or a feeling.

Once, on one of our long walks and trailing behind him, Eric and I couldn't resist the pastries we saw in a *boulangerie*. We went into the shop to buy some. When we came out, Nick was nowhere in sight.

Back at the hotel, he was surprised and puzzled. "Where were you guys? I turned around and you were gone. You ran out on me!"

"We stopped-off for some pastries. You should have been with us. They were great."

Nick and Sheila Paige, his first wife, met as charter members of Actors Inner Circle. They electrified audiences with their powerful stage presence in *The Rainmaker*.

Nick and the author in Nolte's first motion picture, a Disney made-for-TV film called *The Feather Farm*.

Another crazy moment, with Eric in hysterics—"Don't take my picture! Don't take my picture!"

Eric, ready to go before the camera. Producer Ismail Merchant encouraged everyone to be in the film.

Nick and Gwyneth, being readied for the king's entrance, in the Palace of Versailles' famous Hall of Mirrors.

Rehearsal for the presentation of Jefferson's credentials. Nolte hated his wig, even ripping off some offending stray hairs at one point. The director loved the action and kept it in the film.

Gwyneth Paltrow stripping Nick to his Jeffersonian drawers and girdle.

"I can't believe I'm doing this!" she kept screaming. "I can't believe I'm doing this!"

Nick's cry of relief could have been heard in Alaska.
"Aaah-h-h-h!"

A quiet moment with fellow actors and, again, no pants.

Humbert Balsan, co-producer and production manager, got into the act too. Later, he became totally flummoxed by Nick's offer to buy a day from the shooting schedule.

Ismail Merchant the producer, usually warm, pleasant and generous with his time, becomes a demon when anything threatens his budget.

James Ivory, the director, poses with Gwyneth as he waits for a setup to be completed.

Greta Scacchi as Maria Cosway, Jefferson's great love in France.

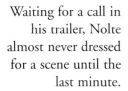

Waiting for a call in his trailer, Nolte almost never dressed for a scene until the last minute.

Gwyneth Paltrow, as sweet and sensitive in real life as she appears in costume.

During the early phases of the shoot, Nick relaxed with extras. Later, he rarely mingled.

Pauline Hayes touches up the precious nose. We were all going to wear one on the last day of the shoot. James Ivory's comment: "You mean we have that many left over? Something went wrong with the budgeting."

Pauline Hayes, guardian of the Jefferson nose, and Betty Glasow, who tended wigs. Not only did they care about Jefferson's appearance, they worried about Nick's emotional well-being.

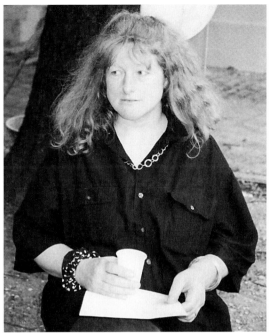

Academy-award-
winning costume
designers Jenny
Beavan and John
Bright came all the
way from England
just for a fitting in
Nolte's house in
Malibu.

In his dressing room, Nick barely tolerated the presence of others as he waited for his calls.

Seth Gilliam, Eric, and Stanislas Robiolle, our patient and thoroughly dependable chauffeur.

Thandie Newton as Sally Hemings, Jefferson's fifteen-year-old slave and the mother of at least one of his children.

Arnaud Borrel

Seth Gilliam as James, Jefferson's other slave in Paris and brother of Sally Hemings.

Nick and Greta worked extremely well together when they came to a scene from the same direction.

Frustrated, French interviewer Kristina never did get the kind of responses she wanted.

Nick often wound up on the floor of my Ritz Hotel room during our wild and hilarious wrestling matches.

Vicki Lewis, Nick's love, is a major talent on her way to stardom. He thought of her constantly during his entire time in Paris.

Johnathon Exley

Nick and Greta in an intimate moment. His fellow actors usually like him and enjoy his rare off-camera appearances.

A replica of the famous Houdon bust of Thomas Jefferson. Nolte's resemblance in costume and make-up was startling.

"I looked all over for you. Then I tried to get home by myself, and I got lost. I wound up hailing a cab. I thought we were taking a walk *together*. You're supposed to let me know when you're going off by yourself."

He was serious. He didn't understand that, true to his fashion, he had really left us long before he felt stranded.

Five

For many actors the first cast-reading of the screenplay takes place in an atmosphere of concern, uncertainty, nervousness and doubt. Who are the other actors? Are they good? Do they know what they're doing? Will they care? Are they going to be there for me? Will I get along with them? Everything is uncertain. Behind the smiles and jokes, everyone watches and measures. It's the first moment of bonding, and it's dramatically important.

Actor relationships are at the heart of their scenes. Harmonious associations generate creativity, and when that harmony is missing, when there's discord instead, then the actors' spirits shrivel, joy disappears, resentments fester in every real and imagined slight, and health—emotional and physical—breaks down. It had recently happened to Nolte with Julia Roberts, and now he approached the gathering of his new colleagues with apprehension.

The first reading of *Jefferson in Paris* took place five days after our arrival in France. Almost all the principals who would share scenes with Thomas Jefferson gathered in one of the smaller conference rooms of the Ritz Hotel.

"I'm going down to the reading now."

"You want me there?"

"No. I'll tell you what happens."

Later I asked, "How'd it go?"

"Great! Jim said the accent's good, and we should all stick to the words."

"Everybody was happy?"

"Yeah. They're all okay. It's going to be a good shoot. I can feel it."

This time the anxiety had been meaningful and realistic. But Nick is experienced enough to know that one reading is never sufficient exposure to gauge his associates accurately. Consequently, there was still some concern. It was a good start, though, and subsequent meetings with Gwyneth Paltrow, who played his daughter Patsy, and Greta Scacchi who played his love interest Maria, tightened bonds so quickly, they fostered a glittering optimism that stoked his interest and charged his batteries.

More than ever before, he was eager to get into costume and to face the cameras. Getting into costume came four days before facing the cameras. Pierre Lhomme, one of France's best directors of photography, requested costume, wig and makeup tests, which would take place at *Château de Chantilly* where they were filming exterior scenes with minor characters. Nolte couldn't wait to get there. The weather was absolutely miserable. Scudding clouds, freezing cold and killing wind. But Nick didn't seem to mind that at all. He was on a positive high. This would be his first time in full costume, wigs and makeup, and he was dying to see how much like Thomas Jefferson they could make him appear.

The "limo" was waiting. "Limousine" to budget-conscious Ismail Merchant defines itself as "suitable car and driver." And in Nolte's case, "suitable car" meant a standard four-door Citroën. Much smaller than the Lincoln Town Cars he's accustomed to, but larger than some tiny Peugeot that Ismail could have foisted upon him. Later, Nick would demand another car for Eric, and after much wrangling he'd get it.

"We can't get along with only one car. I need the back seat for myself. I have to be able to spread out on pillows. I'm not comfortable with someone else back here. I've *never* had someone in the back with me. The back seat's always been mine!"

However, on the day of the test shots, even the size of his car and the fact that I was "squeezed" into the back seat with him couldn't dampen Nolte's enthusiasm.

The driver was a tall, thin, gracious man named Stanislas Robiolle. He spoke the barest of English. He was gentle and pleasant, and though he hadn't been hired for unlimited service, he made himself available to Nolte twenty-four hours a day, every day of the week. With a small child in Normandy to rear, he was desperate for the work.

To Nolte's credit he never abused the driver's willingness to be on endless call. Instead, in the most friendly of ways, he abused the man himself.

"Stanislas. That's a strange name for a Frenchman. I can't call you Stanislas. Do you mind if I call you Stan?"

"No, Meester Nolte."

"And you call me Nick, okay?"

"Okay, Neek."

A sudden, dark explosion and then a contented "Aaaaaaaaaaaahhhhh!"

"Jesus Christ, Nick! Oh, my god! Open your window, Stanislas, *fast*, before he kills all of us!" I cried.

"No," Nick laughed, "leave the windows closed, it's cold out there! It ain't gonna kill ya."

"We're almost dead now! Stanislas, open the damned window!"

Another explosion; another "Aaaaaaaaaahhhhh!"

"Oh, my god!!!" I gasped.

"It's only a little air. What are you getting all excited about? Did you know the human being farts sixteen times a day and swallows half-a-pint of his own mucus? Stan, how do you say fart in French?"

"*Pet*." (Pronounced pay.)

"*Pet*—I like that. Aaaaaaaaaahhhhh!"

"Jesus Christ!!!" I shouted.

"Nick, you're using up your sixteen!" Eric observed.

"He's already used them—one of those is equal to *ten!!* Stanislas, roll down your window!"

Eric and I had ours wide open, but Stanislas remained stoic. He took his orders from Neek and only Neek.

"Close the windows, I'm freezing!" Nick yelled.

We were all freezing. Eric and I had to close ours.

Nolte shook with glee. "Yeahhh!! Stan, how do you say 'great' in French?"

"*Grand*."

"The great fart!"

"*Le grand pet*."

"*Le grand pet*! Yeahhh! *Le grand pet*. Aaaaaaahhhhhh!"

Thereafter, Nick regaled everyone with his story of *le grand pet* and how Stanislas, his driver, was so overwhelmed by his boss's prowess he didn't know whether to faint or die.

They were waiting for Nolte at *Château de Chantilly*—Pauline Hayes and Betty Glasow; they had been brought from England to work on him. Pauline's responsibility through the entire shoot, besides general makeup, would be the Jefferson nose. She'd have to make it a natural appendage, so clean in coloration and connective line that even in tight close-ups the camera would fail to distinguish the prosthetic from the real thing.

Betty's care of the Jefferson wigs demanded equal expertise. Hairline blending, shading, curling and settings would have to deceive the camera, too.

A disheveled Nick Nolte entered the makeup truck, which glittered in bright lights, with drawings and pictures of eighteenth century faces covering the walls and mirrors. And a few hours later, Thomas Jefferson walked out. The effect was amazing. An entirely different head topped the Nolte body. But that wasn't the end of it. An hour later, after he'd been helped into full costume by his dresser, Yann Chadran, he generated enough excitement and glowing exclamations to calm the shakiest of egos. Nolte was an entirely different person now, not only in appearance but in posture and manner as well. He moved about easily as if he'd been transported miraculously back into the realm of France's King Louis XVI. He belonged. And he basked happily in the warmth of everyone's approval.

His own ego reinforced gloriously, he spent the rest of the day waiting for his call, not in the magnificent chateau where he could have passed the time enjoying the splendid art work and decor, but in the isolation of a trailer where he would only read and sleep.

And so began Nick Nolte's location behavior.

During the entirety of a shoot, through all the weeks of actual filming, Nick will remain, for the most part, in the seclusion of his trailer or his dressing room. There, he'll read about his subject, go over his notes endlessly, study his lines, eat ravenously and try to sleep. He will not engage in conversations. He will not do interviews. He will not even allow close associates to be in the same room with him. He will just withdraw until he's called or until his self-imposed solitary confinement palls on him and he feels the restless need of human contact.

The call didn't come until seven o'clock that night. Exterior shooting had been affected by the moody weather, and delays to catch matching light had caused a minor logjam. All the while, Nolte had waited with patience and uncharacteristic grace. Finally, when he was wanted, he strode eagerly to a special area that had been set aside for the test shots, where Pauline and Betty hovered over him, dabbing, touching, constantly correcting what were invisible imperfections to all other eyes.

James Ivory and Pierre Lhomme greeted him with sincere apologies for the delay and with warm appreciation for his patience and understanding.

Nick liked that.

The tests took only minutes. A full day of isolation for a few minutes of testing. That kind of treatment could have made anyone a little edgy, one might believe. But not Nolte. Later, out of costume and makeup and relaxing in the rear seat of the Citroën on his way back to the Ritz Hotel, Nick observed contentedly, "That was good. I like the way it was handled."

What he liked, actually, was not the way everything had been handled, but rather the approval his appearance had stirred. Now, he felt comfortable in the physical form of Thomas Jefferson. He knew he wouldn't look ridiculous. When he saw himself in the makeup and costume mirrors, and he compared his image to the numerous pictures of Jefferson that had been used as references, he'd

been satisfied. More than satisfied—impressed. And
when his own reaction had been supported by the reactions of others, a major point of anxiety had been eliminated. His Thomas Jefferson "look" was now one less
thing to worry about.

But that would be only a temporary period of relief.

The day before that first cast reading at the Ritz Hotel,
Nick received a delightful telephone call.

"Hi, I'm Gwyneth—what are you guys doing now?"

"We're working on some scenes."

"Oooo, cool. Can I come over? I'm going crazy here
all alone."

"Sure, come on over."

"Okay, I'm going to take a shower, and I'll be right
there!"

Gwyneth Paltrow and Nick hadn't met before. But
when they did meet, it was instant chemistry. There was
nothing unusual about this because Gwyneth is an extraordinary woman whose personality, intelligence and wit
can make her lovable even to an ogre. And since Nolte
can be as pleasant and charismatic as a prince when he's
eager to meet someone, her visit had all the essentials for
immediate rapport.

Gwyneth was twenty-one at the time. She is tall, slim
and extremely attractive in a charmingly wispy way. But
more important than the loveliness of her physical
appearance is her energy. She radiates. She will not only
laugh freely at bizarre actions, but she will participate
enthusiastically as well. In coming to the Ritz Hotel to be
with the Nolte Gang she would fuse beautifully. And in
fitting in, she would initiate a fellowship that has lasted

long past the completion of the film.

She breezed into Nick's suite an hour later. There was no hesitancy about her. She was alive with enthusiasm, bright with interest. After Eric and I introduced ourselves, she asked, "You said you're studying scenes—this is my first real part. I don't know what I'm doing. What are you working on? Can I watch?"

"Sure," Nolte agreed. "We'll do something *you're* in. You'll work with us."

"Will I have to do anything? I mean, I won't have to act, will I? 'Cause I'm not ready for that yet."

"No acting. Just talk."

"Oooo, good. Okay, let's go."

Work on a Jefferson-Patsy scene went on for a half-hour. The scene was examined carefully, dissected for its father-daughter significance, probed for its relationship to the entire screenplay, checked for its emotional arc.

Gwyneth was brilliant in her insights. When it was over, we were all elated.

"That was great!" she enthused. "I never knew it could be done that way. Is that what you do all the time?"

"All the time," Nick admitted.

She had seen The Book. "Do you have anything I can take home with me? Some ideas? Some notes?"

"Sure. Eric, give her something to look at."

Eric loaded her down with so much material, we thought it might be overkill.

"I really enjoyed this," she said. "Can we do it again?"

"Any time you want."

After she'd left to return to her apartment, Nolte commented thoughtfully, "That was good."

"*Very* good, Nick," I agreed.

"It's gonna be fun working with her."

"We should do this more often."

"Yeah."

That "yeah" had more in it than pleasure. It had awareness of a critical problem. Since James Ivory doesn't like to direct actors, the Jefferson-Patsy scenes would work better only if he and Gwyneth came to understand their moments together through discussions like the one they'd just enjoyed.

"Who's your favorite director?" I'd once asked Nick.

"There are a few of them. Scorsese, Friedkin, Lumet— a few others."

"Does one stand out a little more than the others?"

"Probably Sidney Lumet."

"Why?"

"He works like a stage director. We put in six weeks of rehearsal before we shot our first foot of film. But when we shot it, we knew exactly what we were doing in every scene. All the characterizations were clearly defined, all the relationships were understood, and all the emotional lines were clearly drawn. It was great. There was agreement all the way around, and the whole shoot went as smooth as butter."

James Ivory doesn't work that way. He and Ismail will say they can't afford that much rehearsal time. The budget won't allow it. But from everything Ivory has said about not presuming to tell an actor anything about his acting, it's more likely that, given the time, he still wouldn't prepare his actors in the way that Nolte finds most gratifying.

It was decided that he and Gwyneth Paltrow would meet on their own and solve their problems themselves.

Two days later, Gwyneth called again.

"I'm going bananas again all alone in this room. I learned a lot the other day. Can I come over and we'll do some more of that?"

"What are you doing there when you should be here?"

"I'll be right over."

This time, she brought her mini-cam with her. "I'm shooting a behind-the-scenes home video for my own memory lane."

Ordinarily, Nolte will balk at any suggestion of having his picture taken under friendly circumstances. He hates it. Literally. His argument is: "Everybody wants to take pictures—paparazzi—interviewers—publicity departments—fans. No pictures, please—I get it from so many other people, my friends, at least, should leave me alone."

But it was different with Gwyneth. With her, there was no objection. And not because he might have been concerned about straining a working relationship by refusing. It was because Gwyneth is…Gwyneth…so open, so friendly, so delightful that refusal was unthinkable.

Eric had been captivated by her, too. And in the course of his thirteen weeks in Paris, his friendship with her strengthened so beautifully that it became one of the safeguards of his emotional stability.

Work that afternoon proved to be so beneficial that Nolte, in one of his expansive moods, suggested we all go out to dinner.

"Good. You pay, Nick," Gwyneth agreed happily. "You're rich."

She called and made reservations at a highly acclaimed restaurant. Her French, though not impeccable, was extremely impressive.

"How long have you been speaking French?" I asked.

"A few weeks. I took a crash course before coming over."

"That's wonderful. I have to learn to speak the language."

"Why?" Nolte asked.

"What do you mean, why? Because it's nice to be able to communicate when you're in a foreign country, that's why."

"Don't waste your time," he advised. "You'll never be good enough to please the French. You're an American. Let them learn to speak English."

That's the way he is wherever he goes. He makes no effort at all to learn another language. He prefers, instead, to fumble his way through to understanding. And that isn't because he's chauvinistic about being American; he feels secure enough about his national identity to admit weaknesses to anyone abroad. Rather, it's because he has a language deficiency. It's nothing serious, but it's there. When Nolte argues something passionately or describes something enthusiastically, it's not with the clear, smooth flow of words that characterize an ease with speech. Instead, his expression is filled with hitches and stammers and wonderful, attention-grabbing malapropisms. His tongue can't always find its way smoothly around certain phrases. It stumbles. More than likely, it's this deficiency that discourages him from learning another language, that makes him believe he can get along best without making the effort. That *and* the fact that, truly, he doesn't have time to squander while he's studying for the next day's work in almost every one of his free moments.

As a result, he gets along very well on location with grunts and body language.

At the restaurant *Le Vaudville* the management was waiting for the Nolte party eagerly. The place was jammed but we were seated almost immediately. The attention seemed to embarrass Nick. He hovered silently and self-consciously at the edge of the group and sank gratefully into his seat in a corner of the room. The stares! The whispers! The smiles! The requests for autographs! The French adore American film stars and they'd been alerted to his presence in Paris by the media; he couldn't escape his celebrity. But it should be acknowledged, he never once displayed displeasure or impatience. He had the Nolte grin and a gracious response for every compliment, and he signed his standard "Best Wishes, Nick Nolte" to every piece of paper extended to him. This was not unusual. Nick is like that in all contacts with the public. Though he detests being recognized, he rarely responds ungraciously. He will give autographs endlessly, stand patiently for paparazzi, and pose to be photographed with fans and their friends or relatives whenever he's asked. I asked him once why he does these things so pleasantly when he'd really rather not be bothered. He just smiled and answered somewhat plaintively, "It comes with the business."

The dinner at *Le Vaudeville* was exceptional. Besides a lentil-mushroom salad, fine wines, delicious breads, taste-refreshing sorbets and incredible desserts, we were served extraordinary entrées. Nick and Eric devoured a glorious veal preparation that was as good in artistic appearance as it was in flavor; Gwyneth consumed an entire chateaubriand; and I went wild over delicately sauced filet of trout upon a bed of spinach, mushrooms and spiced rice.

What made the evening even more enjoyable was the conversation. When we weren't laughing at jokes and witty repartee, we talked about everything from sexual experiences to secret feelings. Gwyneth had an endless stream of questions. When was the first time you masturbated? Do you think Thomas Jefferson and his daughter had an incestuous relationship? What do you think of Merchant and Ivory? Do you like them? Have you ever been deeply affected by the sudden death of a friend?

"Yeah," Nick said. "His name was Rocky. He was sweet and innocent and always in trouble because he just didn't fit."

"Did you miss him?"

"Yeah."

"Do you still miss him?"

"I think about him sometimes."

"And what about marriage? How many times have you been married?"

"Three."

"What were they like?"

He described each of his wives.

"You're getting divorced from Rebecca now, aren't you?"

"Trying to. It's rough. We even went to this psychiatrist, who's supposed to be the best in the world. He doesn't see actors because, he says, they trick him too often. But he saw me after I promised to talk only about Brawley. He gave me advice: 'Don't fight in the divorce; it'll destroy the boy.' So we're trying to do this sensibly, but it's rough."

"If you could take one of your wives to a dinner like this right now, which would you choose?"

"Probably Sheila. I think that would be interesting."

The answer suggested a secret feeling that hadn't been resolved and more than likely hasn't been resolved even to this day. Knowing Nolte and Sheila intimately, and remembering their tempestuous years together, I couldn't help thinking *Yes, indeed, that certainly would be interesting.*

A memorable dinner.

However, all French food while we were in Paris wasn't that enjoyable. Actually, some of it on the sets of *Jefferson in Paris* was so fat saturated that for survival I had one of the assistants teach me how to say "Please, I'm a vegetarian. Is it possible to give me four hot vegetables and some bread?"

"I told you," Nolte scoffed as I achieved perfect French pronunciation. "It won't do you any good. They're only gonna laugh at you."

What came out of this is another Nolte story that he loves to tell.

Ending one of our walks one day on the Right Bank, we stopped at a little café for lunch. The place was empty. We seated ourselves. The waiter, a thin man whose singular expression included a constantly raised eyebrow, approached our table with menus.

"*Monsieur*," he said, handing one to Nick.

Nolte took it without a word.

"*Monsieur*," he said, handing me the other.

"*Merci*," I said, and Nick shook his head and made a face.

The menus were entirely in French. No English translations.

The waiter stood by with pad and pencil poised. Suddenly, Nolte's hand shot up before the man's face, fist clenched, index finger pointing rigidly. The waiter jumped in surprise but regained his composure quickly. He raised his other eyebrow questioningly, half-closed his eyelids and tilted his head.

Nick rotated his index finger vigorously right under the man's nose and then plunged it at the menu.

Understanding flickered in the waiter's expression. He looked closely at where Nolte's finger had stopped and made a note on his pad.

Nick did this three times. He had absolutely no idea what he was ordering. He didn't even care. His finger was speaking for him.

When he had finished with the menu-stabber, the waiter turned to me.

I leaned back in my chair confidently, and in my best French reeled off my practiced vegetarian litany. It was greeted with a torrent of French, a veritable deluge that almost drowned me. I couldn't understand a word of it. All I could do was smile somewhat helplessly. And to keep from looking like a complete idiot, I nodded with assurance and answered, "*Oui*."

The waiter nodded his head and smiled. In time, he returned with food. He placed Nolte's order before him and disappeared.

With the Goddess of Luck guiding his finger, Nick had ordered a wonderful lunch, and from the way he grunted as he ate, it was as good as it looked.

I waited.

Nothing came.

"What are they doing," I grumbled to Nick, "growing the vegetables?"

He became a little sardonic. "Your French is so good, they're probably preparing the specialty of the house for you."

I waited.

And still nothing came.

Finally, beyond patience, and with Nolte grinning

and grunting his pleasure, I signaled the waiter and caught his attention.

"*Oui, Monsieur?*" The eyebrow was raised again.

At a loss for the correct words and not daring to try my vegetarian request again, I asked rather helplessly, "Is there...anyone here...who speaks...English...?"

"Certainly, *Monsieur.* I do. And very well, if I must say."

I thought Nick would choke.

"All right...okay...where's my lunch? Why's he been served and I haven't?"

"Oh, *Monsieur*, I am so sorry, but when you ordered, I said to you, 'You seem to be having some difficulty with my language. Perhaps *Monsieur* would like to think a little longer about what he wishes,' and you said, '*Oui*.'"

Nolte settled back and flashed his most comically smug, I-told-you-so grin.

No lunch that day. But there was plenty of Nick's laughter—all the way back to the hotel and every chance he got to describe how beautifully foolish I'd looked and how his stiff finger instinctively knew better French than my practiced tongue would ever manage.

Six

There were 141 scenes in Ruth Jhabvala's screenplay.

Thomas Jefferson would appear in 69, almost all of them major moments of the action. And Nick would suffer through every one of them.

In motion picture production, budgetary considerations make sequential scheduling virtually impossible. The need to shoot everything in a particular location while it's still available scrambles the screenplay's scenes. It becomes difficult for the actor to sustain his line of thinking and his emotional continuity. In a good screenplay, each scene follows logically from the preceding scene. All build emotionally and intelligently to meaningful climaxes. In the schedule, nothing follows logically, and climaxes occur in meaningless disorder. Conscientious actors approach their scenes, then, with great trepidation, wondering if they'll be able to grasp the moment's emotional significance without the benefit of sequential development.

Being more than conscientious—being downright possessed—Nolte moves from day to day in constant anxiety, which in a very short time becomes withering, deadly panic. No amount of discussion can ease his concerns.

He's a worrier. And he will admit this readily with a charming, self-deprecating laugh. However, no one but his assistant will ever see his fears. Outside his hotel suite and his dressing room he will appear to be calm, relaxed and in full control of what he feels he'll be required to do. But away from other eyes, he becomes tense, impatient, curt and even sullen in his uncertainty.

In eighteenth century Paris, Franz Anton Mesmer had captured the fancy of the French aristocracy. Even Marie Antoinette expressed interest in his hypnotism gatherings and the alleged healing powers of his "Animal Magnetism."

The first scene in which Nick was to go before the cameras would occur nine days after he'd landed at Charles de Gaulle Airport. It would depict one of Mesmer's remarkable seances. It was a strong scene, showing the power of suggestion, the gullibility of sophistication and the piercing honesty of Jefferson's intellect. In the screenplay, it appears midway through the script, the logical result of preceding events. Before the camera, it had no such foundation. As the twelfth of April drew closer, Nolte's anxiety intensified. We discussed the scene endlessly. And right up to the moment of his call, he ran his lines and reviewed his notes again and again, never really believing he was prepared adequately for the shot.

"Okay, Nicholas, that does it. You've got it."

"Don't *say* that! I don't have it!"

"You've got it."

"Don't ever tell me I've got it because I *never* get it!"

"That's bullshit. I know when you understand something, and you do too. You've got it."

"*Jesus Christ!* Why do you have to upset me this way?!"

"I don't upset you. You upset yourself. Would it make you feel more secure if I say you *don't* have it?"

"Yes!"

"Okay then, you don't have it. Feel better?"

"Yes!…No!…Leave me alone, will ya? I can't deal with you now! I want to be by myself!"

The day had started at 6:00 A.M. with breakfast on the set; rehearsals would begin at 8:00 A.M.; shooting would commence at 9:00, and the day's wrap would be 8:00 P.M. Twelve hours of work within a fourteen-hour day. And this would be the basic schedule through the entire shoot. Of course, variations and modifications would be dictated by necessity but, in the main, a fourteen-hour day that could produce two-and-a-half minutes of usable footage would be considered a successful day's work.

The Mesmer scene was shot at Versailles, not at the palace, but nearby at the *Hôtel Forquenot de la Fortelle*, an ancient building within a group of contemporary structures and busy streets. It took the entire day to film a little more than one page of the screenplay, but after twelve hours, it had been shot from every conceivable angle and with every necessary close-up. James Ivory seemed satisfied; the scene conveyed the drama, comedy and significance he'd hoped to capture. Ismail Merchant was pleased; the scene had been completed on schedule and progress, so far, was within budget. And Nick Nolte, despite his fears, considered it a very successful first day.

However, film making in Ivory's words, "…is a matter of bits and pieces," and though he was satisfied with Nick's first day, he was still not entirely certain that he'd made the correct choice in selecting him to be Thomas Jefferson. Everything seemed right—the appearance, the voice, the Jeffersonian temperament—but as important as it was, the Mesmer scene had been only a "bits and pieces" day's work. Something more substantial, more demanding, was needed to put the director's final doubts to rest.

That "something" took place three days later at *Basilique St. Denis*, approximately eight kilometers from the heart of Paris.

Its steeples and spires may not rival the impressive architecture of *Notre-Dame* but *St. Denis* surpasses Paris's most famous cathedral with what it has inside. Because that's where almost all of France's royalty is interred in row upon row of marble sarcophagi, their sides decorated with ornate friezes and their covers bearing life-size sculptures of the kings and queens entombed therein.

And it was in the darkness of the night, in an eerily lighted area, that Thomas Jefferson would describe his love for his dead wife Martha to his new love Maria Cosway.

Again, Nolte approached the scene with his customary anxiety.

"I don't know where Greta's gonna come from with this," he worried. "I wish we were in agreement. We could play off each other better that way. This way we may be going in different directions. I wish we'd had rehearsals."

"If you feel that way, call her, ask her to come over, and we'll go over the scene with her the way we did with Gwyneth."

"You think she'll agree?"

"All she can say is no."

But Greta Scacchi didn't say no. As a matter of fact, being as interested as Nolte in doing outstanding work, she thought a meeting with him was an excellent idea.

We sat in Nolte's suite; Nick worked from his notes in The Book, and the discussion went something like this:

"We meet eleven times in the screenplay. *St. Denis* is

only the third time."

"So at this point, Nick, we're just getting to know each other."

"Right. The love is just starting. I'm taking it from this direction: all eleven meetings that we have add up to a full statement of what love is, how it works and why it can be blocked-off when it isn't understood."

"Then at this early stage in *St. Denis* what you're really doing is telling me what you think true love is as opposed to the romantic kind that everyone in France is practicing?"

"Exactly."

"But I'm seeing a sensitive part of you that I find very touching, so my feelings for you are strengthened intensely by your revelations."

"I'm using my marriage to Martha as an example of real love—"

"In order to lay the foundation for the relationship between you and me."

"Exactly."

"This is a very precious and delicate moment between us, Nick."

"It has to be."

"I tell you very intimate things about myself, which deepens your feelings for me, too. We'll be seeing *into* each other for the first time."

"And if we don't, Greta, then our whole love after this won't work."

"The love affair falls apart anyway, Nick."

"Yes, but that's because real love and romantic love don't mix."

"But that suggests Maria isn't capable of real love. I don't like that."

"She's capable of it—*very* capable—but she'd have to give up everything she is and owns in Europe to come to America with him, and she's too much of the Old World to do that."

"I like that. So, tell me, according to Jefferson, what is real love as opposed to romantic love?"

The meeting lasted over an hour but when it was over, both Nick and Greta had reached agreement on the meaning of the scene and how they were going to approach it.

"Feel better?" I asked him after she had left.

"Yes."

"You should—because you have it."

"Don't say that! Don't *say* that!" he erupted, but this time he smiled as he shook his head.

It would be a critical scene. Historically recognized as an extremely reserved and reticent person, Jefferson would be revealed now as a tender and sensitive man with an ability to convey deeper meanings through personal experiences. It would also convey his sense of privacy, his capacity to love and his willingness to share his most cherished memories, under certain circumstances, with another human being. In short, it would humanize him.

Now, in the Gothic stillness of *St. Denis*, its eeriness in perfect harmony with the texture of the moment, Nolte and Scacchi met before the camera for the first time. And the scene worked. So beautifully, in fact, that everyone watched almost without breathing.

When the evening ended, James Ivory sighed with satisfaction and relief. "If that's not Thomas Jefferson," he said softly to me, "then *nobody* is."

Later, he remarked, "In the Mesmer scene, Nick didn't have that much to do. But at *St. Denis* he really had to

do something challenging in a way that would be rewarding to watch as it was being done. There at *St. Denis* it
was possible to judge the performance. It was a piece that
was long enough and had all kinds of mood changes, and
as I watched him I saw that this was going to be fine. At
that point, I knew he and we were on the right track."

The director's pleasure was made known to Nolte.
Did it please him? Unquestionably. Did it make him feel
more secure? Not in the least. As the days passed, each
scene was approached with the same fears, the same driving need to grasp a shimmering perfection that was
always out of his reach. And the effort exhausted him.

"What's this exhaustion all about?" I asked. "You
work a few hours a day, you sit in your dressing room and
rest most of the time, when you do come out you're pampered and catered to like a king, and when you're actually on the set in front of the cameras you become God. So
what's there to knock you out? Why're you so damned
tired all the time?"

He responded with an explanation that could be
titled "Carefully Considered Conclusions on the Actor's
Biological Reactions to the Demands of Film Making" or,
to be succinct, "The Nolte Adrenaline Theory."

"You don't understand," Nick said. "Film acting isn't
like stage acting. In stage acting, you work yourself up to
a full performance. The adrenaline starts pumping, it's
sustained for two hours, and you're on a high throughout
the whole show. In film, it's entirely different. You have to
work yourself up to a scene. The adrenaline starts pumping. The scene lasts only minutes, not two hours. Then
there's that drop-off until the next take, which is sometimes only minutes away, and then you work the adrenaline up again and you're on a terrific high, and then it

drops off again. And this goes on all day, every day. That up-and-down, up-and-down, that adrenaline elevator, can wipe you out. After a stage performance when the adrenaline's been working for two hours, you have a chance to rest and recover. But after a whole day of that elevator in film acting, there's no recovery—at least not for me. So eventually it catches up with me and I'm exhausted. The only time it ends is when the shooting ends. And until that happens, I have to conserve my strength by not socializing too much and by resting as much as I can."

Of course, as with many theories, Nolte's argument has a gaping hole. Stage acting doesn't require actors to be onstage all the time; often they sit backstage or in the greenroom waiting for their next entrance, just as the film actor has to wait for his next take or setup. There should be no more of an adrenaline demand in film work, then, than there is in stage performance. Nolte shouldn't become exhausted during every film for this reason. His explanation satisfies him, though. And he would become quite agitated if it were ever challenged.

I suspect the real reason he becomes so tired all the time is something he may not be willing to face squarely yet, although he's danced around it often in our discussions. It may be simply that he's reaching the point of burnout. He takes almost no pleasure in his work now. It has become brutal, demanding, something that for the most part generates complaints. There's little joy, little feeling of success. He never really appreciates the immediacy of accomplishment. By the time a completed film comes out, it's almost forgotten because he's halfway through another one. No film is truly rewarding as it's being made. All he can experience is some momentary satisfaction in doing the individual scenes. But now even that brief pleasure is no longer there for him to any significant degree. He's doing what he supposedly loves. Well, love has happiness, joy, and even ecstasy in it. Obviously, if the work doesn't generate these emotions, there's no real love for it anymore. There's only habit and a kind of self-delusion about the love of acting.

He's a prisoner of his own efforts. Acting is what he does best, and the expensive structure that his work has enabled him to construct in his life *requires* more acting just to sustain it. In addition to this is the disturbing truth that he wouldn't know what to do with himself if he were *not* acting.

It's sad. He's trapped. And he hasn't consciously recognized his *un*happiness yet in doing something that, at one time, produced only the pleasure of involvement and the joy of success.

Nevertheless, his Adrenaline Theory seems to work for him. When he's on a set, as tired as he may be before a shot, somehow, from somewhere, he pulls a rush of energy from the core of his being and rises beautifully to the demands of the scene.

This is not to say he's incapable of enjoyment or that there are absolutely no moments of fun for him. He still slips into spontaneous bursts of idiocy that convulse onlookers and cause him no end of pleasure. At these times, he's the center of all attention, totally free of inhibition and liberated from his weariness. And in that freedom he creates situations that are so funny they remain indelibly in the minds of anyone fortunate enough to have been with him at that time.

For example—

Every morning before leaving his hotel for the set, Nolte would have room service deliver a full breakfast while he was taking his bath. He needs food quickly to start his day. One might imagine that a hearty breakfast would have satisfied this need. Well, it did—but only until he reached the set. There, because everyone else was having breakfast, Nick believed he needed *another* full meal. So every day, he ate two breakfasts *and* a huge lunch, which was delivered from the hotel, *and* snack food and fruits, *and* something from room service upon returning for the night.

In a very short time he'd gained enough weight to make him believe his magnificent costumes had become Iron Maidens. His girdle strangled him now from the waist up. He felt as if he were choking. His trousers had become skin-tight. He had trouble sitting in them. His shirts and waistcoats had become straitjackets. Binding. Restrictive. Downright stultifying. And even his feet hurt in shoes that now had Heels from Hell.

His patient and even-tempered dresser, Yann, was being driven crazy by Nick's loud and comical pleas for release from these demon clothes the moment he entered his dressing room. But one day Yann wasn't there when Nick came off the set.

"Where's Yann? I need Yann. Where's Yann? Oh God, get me *out* of these things!"

He charged into a waiting room where Gwyneth, Pauline, Eric and I were sitting and talking.

"Yann! *Yann!* Has anybody seen *Ya-a-a-nn*?!"

"What's the matter?" Gwyneth asked, concerned.

"I gotta get out of these pants! I'm dying! Get me out of these pants! Somebody, get me out of these pants! Patsy, *help!*"

Gwyneth responded as a loving daughter would. She hurried to him and grabbed the sides of his Jefferson pants.

"Faster! Faster! I'm going! I'm going! I'm not gonna make it!"

Gwyneth tugged wildly.

Nick fell to the floor and raised his legs. "Faster! Faster!"

Gwyneth pulled insanely and dragged him halfway across the room as Nick grunted and groaned so ridiculously the rest of us almost collapsed in hysteria. Even Nick and Gwyneth had to laugh.

"I can't believe I'm doing this!" she screamed. "*I can't believe I'm doing this!*"

But she persisted until the pants came off; and when they did, the sob of relief from Nolte was so comical it could have made even Pagliacci forget his grief. And all of us were left with the unforgettable picture of an impeccably attired Thomas Jefferson, groaning and writhing on the floor while his daughter worked madly to strip him to his drawers.

At another time:

"This may be my first X-rated movie," James Ivory said. He was smiling but there was a touch of concern in his voice and in the slight embarrassment of his glance.

The location was the *Palais Royale* in the heart of Paris. A corner of the site had been redesigned and decorated to reproduce the remarkable shopping center of Jefferson's day.

In its original form, the *Palais Royale* offered Parisians almost everything they could desire: a subterranean circus with equestrian performances; restaurants; theaters; stores of every imaginable kind; art galleries; rooms for chess tournaments; places to demonstrate new inventions. Everything.

But most appreciated and universally anticipated were

the puppet shows. It was the puppet show that was now troubling James Ivory.

Queen Marie Antoinette was believed to be having an affair with one of her kinsmen. Though she was considered to be rather promiscuous, her liaisons with other men were cause only for mild gossip. But because of the incestuous nature of *this* one, there was a lot more radical commentary. At any rate, the affair became the subject of *Palais Royale* puppet shows. And it was enacted in the most graphic and exaggerated terms of the day. Huge red penises in gargantuan erections. Naked bottoms. Stunning copulation gyrations. Nothing was left to the imagination.

Later, when a discussion arose about the obscene nature of the puppet show, Nolte stated his belief that James Ivory was worrying for nothing, that puppetry is always so enjoyable in itself, it would strip the scene entirely of its objectionable obscenity.

"When puppets are involved," Nick explained, "people are so captivated, they don't see obscenity."

That was a strong statement and it stirred strong disagreement. The discussion continued, hot and heavy. Nick left it. He turned away and walked to a corner of the room. In a few minutes he returned. But this time the fly of his Jefferson trousers was down, his shirttail was wrapped around his penis like a shawl, and the head of his organ was wearing a comical face that he'd drawn with a black pen.

The women screamed. They couldn't believe he was actually flashing himself. The laughter became a roar. It isn't every day you see Thomas Jefferson whipping his penis around like a puppet.

"Hello Ladies," Nolte said in a crazy, squeaky voice as

he poked his "puppet" toward the women. "What's the matter, don't you want to say hello to me?"

The laughter could have been heard in London.

"Don't you want to be my friend?" he asked.

"No, I don't want to be your friend," Gwyneth answered, looking directly at the "puppet" and not at Nick.

And that started it.

A remarkable conversation took place between Nick's penis and all the women in the room, a conversation so wild and witty it had everyone choking on laughter. They were talking to it. They were actually talking to it! They'd completely forgotten all their earlier statements about obscenity. They'd been taken in entirely by the magic of his "puppetry."

And Nick grinned triumphantly as he put his penis back into his pants. "See?" he said. "No obscenity."

He'd enjoyed himself immensely in that moment; so much, he said he might even give some press interviews that way. "Y'know, get a little jacket for him and a tiny three-cornered hat. Maybe even a little red wig."

Indeed, though he grows progressively mad as the days of filming pass, nothing will ever completely destroy Nolte's wonderful sense of humor.

Seven

From the first day of his arrival in France, Nick's love affair with Vicki began to shape itself as a critical instrument for his survival. Vicki became his lifeline to sanity. He didn't talk *about* her very much. But he spoke *to* her endlessly. Not a day went by that they failed to connect in telephone calls that sometimes lasted hours. And often, in a flash of needing, even as we drove to the set for a day's work, he'd grab his international cellular and dial her in New York just to say hello and to enjoy a few words.

Nick's telephone bills ran into thousands of dollars. That was of no consequence, though. The calls uplifted him. That's what counted. They gave him a feeling that he was being loved, that someone far away from the isolation and the life-sapping work on the film was truly caring about him, worrying about him, wrapping him in the comforting warmth of her love. And needing that, he released himself more and more to feelings that, under normal circumstances, he's never fully trusted. He not only allowed himself to fall in love, he actually charged into it.

Loneliness and long-distance contact often encourage

the hunger, the yearning, of love.

They made plans.

Vicki's contract with *Damn Yankees* was going to expire around the time that work on *Jefferson in Paris* would be completed. She decided not to renew. Since Nick was determined to take a long vacation before even reading another screenplay, she'd leave New York for LA and move in with him for a four-month trial.

The prospect excited Nick. It gave him something to look forward to, something to hold onto, and he couldn't wait to see her again. His contract with Merchant Ivory included two trips to Paris by Concorde for a wife or companion. He wouldn't have to wait for the four-month trial period to see Vicki again. Nolte prepared himself for Vicki's first visit.

"She'll be here soon."

"For how long?" I asked.

"She has a week's vacation coming to her."

"That's great. Will she be staying the whole week?"

"We don't know yet."

"It'll give both of you a chance to work some things out about her move to LA"

"Yeah. She really wants to make the move. She told me yesterday she's turned down an offer to do a revival of *Funny Girl* on Broadway."

"*Really?*"

"They want her for the lead."

"And she turned it down?"

"She kept saying no and, you know the business, every time you say no the offer goes up. They were up to fifteen thousand a week before they finally understood she meant what she was saying."

"That's a hell of a thing to turn down. It could make

her a Broadway superstar."

"She'd rather be with me."

"And how does that make *you* feel?"

"What do you mean?"

"She's giving up a terrific opportunity. How does that make you feel?"

"It's her decision."

"But you know what that could mean for her career. If *Funny Girl* were to succeed, you could move to New York for a few months to be with *her*. And if it bombs, she could move out to LA then and never have to wonder about *what-ifs*. But if she goes out to LA without trying it at all, *what-if* may dog her for the rest of her life."

"It's her decision."

"And don't you give her input?"

"No."

Nolte likes to believe that his dedication to individual freedom extends into all relationships, that no one has the right to make life-governing demands upon another human being. It's a noble belief. One that engenders the loftiest expression of mutual respect. However, in actuality, Nick uses it very often for self-serving purposes. He will give all kinds of advice in matters that don't impinge upon his own needs. But he'll abstain from counseling when advice may cause him to do something that he really doesn't care to do. In this case, living in New York with Vicki for a few months, or possibly a year, wasn't as desirable as having her move out to Malibu to be with *him*. And the reason for that is that, out of his Hollywood habitat, Nolte feels like a lion in the desert: he can get along but not like an animal more indigenous to the terrain. Broadway is not his terrain. So he allowed the decision to be entirely hers.

When Vicki arrived in Paris, she and I spoke about that decision.

"How do you feel about it?" I asked.

"Truthfully? A little angry. I even told him, 'Look what I'm giving up for you.' My friends think I'm crazy. But I want a life. I want marriage and children. My clock is ticking. I love Nick, and I want to be with him."

I didn't want to say, "You could still be with him if he were willing to be with *you* in New York." However, it was clear from the way she spoke that the thought was in her mind.

Their week together in Paris wasn't as idyllic as both had hoped. Not because they didn't connect. They did—extremely well. When they weren't in bed making love, they were either matching wits happily or talking seriously. But always with warmth and mutual affection. The problem was work, Nolte's schedule. It never allowed the continuity that both of them desired. And Nolte was always concerned that running around Paris with Vicki might further deplete his precarious energies. As a result she didn't see very much of the city, and she often felt that going to the set of *Jefferson in Paris* and having to wait for a take to end in order to see him for only a few minutes was time that could have been better spent.

Nevertheless her first visit strengthened their love and buoyed Nick's spirit considerably. She had made it pleasanter for everyone else to be near him. For a time after Vicki returned to New York he laughed more easily and he became playful again, playful enough even to transform serious media interviews into other ridiculous Nolte comedies.

Ismail Merchant, ever conscious of marketing techniques for his projects, had arranged to have a cameraman and an interviewer on the various sets for weeks, taping and questioning everyone for a planned How-the-Film-Was-Made video. The cameraman was a tall, quiet technician who went by the name of Thomas; the interviewer was a sweet, kittenish Frenchwoman by the name of Kristina. They had interviewed everyone connected in any significant way with the production. Everyone, that is, except Nick Nolte. And the video, of course, would be worthless without his presence. They had been trying desperately to corner him. But Nick had avoided them at every turn. Their pleas went ignored. Their schemes floundered. But after Vicki left Paris, Nick's resistance weakened one day between takes and he allowed the video camera to roll.

Since Kristina had been so spectacularly unsuccessful in getting Nick to answer questions, she thought it might be more comfortable for him if someone else were to do the interview, someone closer to him. She importuned Gwyneth to do the questioning for her. And Gwyneth agreed enthusiastically. Kristina, of course, had chosen the wrong person because the Nolte-Gwyneth relationship had become much too friendly to produce any kind of seriousness.

The interview would take place in Nolte's dressing room.

The camera was set up. Nolte lay on his couch. Gwyneth crouched at his side, her head near his head, the microphone in her hand. And Kristina and Thomas stood expectantly at the side, their hopes raised high by Nolte's sudden willingness. *Finally*, they would complete their assignment.

"Nick, how did you prepare for your role of Thomas Jefferson?" Gwyneth started.

His manner became dignified, contemplative, even presidential, and it remained that way throughout the session.

"It was very easy. I put a false nose on and knew I was very sexy because the nose is a symbol of the male organ, and the longer the nose, the bigger the organ. With this nose, I'm *very* sexy."

"C'mon, answer the question."

"I'm telling you the truth."

"You're an idiot."

Thomas and Kristina were bewildered. But they continued to hope and to tape.

"And then I passed wind—a long, beautiful *grand pet.*"

"C'mon, answer me!"

"Did you know you pass wind an average of sixteen times a day? I tell that to everybody. We should all be aware of it!"

"I do not."

"Yes, you do."

"I don't!"

"Everybody does."

"Not me."

Thomas and Kristina knew they were helpless now; the interviewer had gone over to the other side.

"Why are you afraid to admit it? Flatulence is a natural bodily function. It's healthy. It lubricates the intestines and allows the bowels to flow freely."

"N-i-i-ck!"

"It does! And then you don't get constipation. One of the worst things that can happen to you is not being able to move your bowels. Everyone knows that."

"No shit." And Gwyneth laughed.

"Right!" And Nolte laughed, too.

"All right, tell me, did Thomas Jefferson ever pass wind?"

"Absolutely! Jefferson was the greatest farter of them all. That's why he's called The Farter of Our Country."

"That was Washington, you imbecile!"

"Yes, but he taught Washington everything he knew!"

"And it was father not farter."

"No. It was farter, but people like you who are afraid to admit they do that *thing*, changed it to father."

As if on cue, Nolte then produced a rip-roaring explosion of gas.

"Oooohh—he farted on me! You're so *gross*! He *farted* on me!"

Thomas and Kristina could only look stupified and defeated. However, worrying about having an incomplete assignment on their hands, they tried valiantly again a few minutes later, only this time it was on the set with Greta Scacchi asking the questions.

Of course Greta had no more success with Nick than Gwyneth had had. All of his answers to her questions were preposterous responses that clearly showed his antipathy to any kind of interview situation. But suddenly, for no explicable reason, Nolte began to describe the Jefferson-Maria Cosway love affair in lucid, orderly and intelligent terms.

"Well…" Greta said quietly and obviously impressed. "The other side of Nick Nolte. He *can* get serious."

She tried to continue in the same mood, but he switched back swiftly into the absurd again. When she protested, he kept demanding more questions until Greta threw up her hands and pleaded, "Mel, you interview him."

"No, thank you. You're doing fine."

"Please. Maybe you know how to get something sensible out of this man."

"C'mon, ask me a question! C'mon! C'mon! I'm ready, I'm ready! Make it a good one!"

Greta had surrendered. It was evident that no question would satisfy him. He was having too much fun. A serious question would surely have fed his fires. So I took the microphone from her and started with something asinine.

"All right, Mister Nolte, American and International movie star, whose fame has spread to Mars, Jupiter and all points of the—"

"For chrissake, what's your question? Jesus, ask him to ask a question, and he has to make a speech! That's the way he *always* is. He has to make a speech about everything!"

He had everyone laughing, even Thomas and Kristina.

"All right, Mister Jefferson, a quick question—"

"Finally!"

"A wonderful woman has just gone back to America. How many times have you had sex in the past week?"

His expression became deadly serious. Silently, slowly, he began to count his fingers.

"Would you like to remove your shoes, sir?"

He grinned comically; everyone was roaring.

The interview ended on that note and, of course, Thomas and Kristina still had little or nothing they could use. And for whatever reason, though Nolte did grant a couple of serious interviews in the course of the production—one to a British video team and the other to the Smithsonian Institution magazine—I believe Thomas and Kristina never did get anything of real value from him.

Vicki's visit had invigorated Nick. And their week together had been beneficial to his health, to his performance before the camera and, for a while, to everyone who had to work closely with him.

It was around this time that matters with Rebecca began to intrude upon his emotional stability. Believing that they were actually coming to some kind of agreement on a final divorce settlement, he was thrown unexpectedly into a quagmire of despair. Rebecca had begun to insist upon alimony. This time, distance didn't nourish fond feelings. Instead, it intensified a feeling of helplessness. And his transatlantic telephone calls to her were charged with frustration. He took his stand: *no alimony!* He believed he had given enough. He'd agreed to an even split of their assets; he'd agreed to child support; he'd even agreed to a share of royalties from his previous pictures. But there would be no alimony!

"I'm not going to tie myself in a straitjacket for the rest of my life," he explained to me. "I'll be forced to work just to meet the alimony payments. What if I don't want to work anymore? What if I decide to retire? I don't want that weight around my neck for the rest of my life! We've been trying to avoid legal battles all along, but if she insists on alimony, I'll take this whole thing right into the courtroom."

After weeks of discussion and argument, the matter was finally resolved. Nick had won his point. But not before the bitterness of the dispute had corroded more of his fading patience and dwindling strength.

As Nolte grows impatient or feels his strength declining, he becomes more difficult than ever. Graciousness disappears. Ordinary courtesy goes. He begins to demand things; he begins to imagine problems that don't exist; and as real problems develop, he becomes downright paranoid.

One morning, Eric brought him his second breakfast. He was seated on his couch in a small room, which had been set up as a makeup room for him, and which he preferred to the makeup trailer because it satisfied his need for privacy. He accepted the plate of greasy bacon and eggs and ordered, "Give me that chair over there. I need a table."

It was Betty's chair. She wasn't using it at the moment, but that didn't matter. There had been no "May I use your chair, Betty?" No "Please bring me that chair, Eric." Just a curt, "Give me that chair over there, I need a table," as if some lordly right made everything his.

Eric pulled the chair over to him.

Nick put his plate on it and dug into his breakfast. When he was through eating, he allowed the chair to be returned to Betty, and Eric left the room to find him a table. While he was gone, Nolte accidentally spilled some orange juice on the floor. Whereupon, Pauline began to sop it up with a Kleenex.

"Where the hell's my table?" Nick bawled. "I need a table. Eric takes off and I'm spilling things because he hasn't found me a table."

At that moment, Eric returned with a small table.

"Oh, good," Nick breathed. "I need that."

No "thank you." No "I can always count on you, Eric." No kindness or appreciation of any sort.

One scene had Maria Cosway visiting Jefferson at his *de*

Langeac home in Paris with the explanation that she had returned from London to be with him. The meeting takes place in Jefferson's music room, near the harpsichord. After three takes, while adjustments were being made, Nolte walked anxiously off the set.

"Follow me, will you?"

It had been requested in a troubled whisper.

We went upstairs to his dressing room. He closed the door.

"What do you think?"

"About what?"

"The scene. How's it going?"

"It's going beautifully."

"You don't think I'm being squeezed out? I mean, everything seems to be focused on Greta. Like they're giving her the scene."

"They're not giving her anything. It *is* her scene."

"I'm starting to feel like I'm there just to help everybody, like this isn't about Jefferson at all."

"You're crazy. The scene is beautiful."

"But she's facing the camera and you don't see me."

"Nick—first, the scene is hers. She comes to *de Langeac* to tell you something that could change everyone's life, that could have changed the world. If she had gone with you to Monticello, you would never have become president and all of history would be different today. Of course, that's not part of the scene. Nobody knows that. But the point is, what she's come to tell you is very important to her and to you, too. She's the thrust of the scene. That makes the scene hers."

"You don't think I'm being wiped out by the angle?"

"No way. The blocking is perfect. Jim has her seated on the harpsichord bench; you're standing, towering over her. Your position is dominant. He has to have her the way she is or you'll take the scene away from her. So to get the balance, he turns her toward the camera a little more than you. It's perfect, it's beautiful, and you're being crazy again."

"Yeah, that makes sense. Okay. Whew—pull me back together whenever I get this way, will you?"

Exhaustion makes Nolte imagine things, which often cause him to feel he's being slighted. However, instead of discussing the problem with his director he will avoid what could become confrontation and seek reassurance on less dangerous ground. If there's no one available whom he can trust, he'll sulk silently then and work himself into a fit of depression. Can he control it? No.

"It happens on every film," he'll insist. "And it happens to everyone."

"Well, if it makes everybody so unhappy, you ought to study it and try to get rid of it."

"We can't. It's uncontrollable. It's part of acting in films. We begin to see things that aren't there. We can't avoid it. It's the craziness."

In fairness to Nick, his belief that madness develops in *everyone* on *all* productions has a great deal of validity. As unforeseen problems arise (difficulties that affect the shooting schedule and the budget), personalities undergo startling changes. Ordinarily even-tempered people begin to complain about trifles, like having to wait for a camera setup or not being informed about minor changes in routine. In time they turn upon each other and vent their frustrations with vituperation and even ludicrous threats. Sometime they try to mask their irritation with smiles or with a tenuous laugh. But everyone knows that behind the camouflage something real and dangerous is seething.

No one is immune. And although his attacks were never truly vicious, producer Ismail Merchant even turned upon his dear friend and partner, director James Ivory.

"Wigs! Wigs! More fucking wigs! Every picture we do has to have your fucking wigs! We carry the fucking wigs around with us like fucking garbage! Let's make a fucking picture for once without your fucking wigs! Jim, we cannot go over another fucking day! I will not sign another fucking check, do you hear?! Not another fucking check! If we go over another fucking day, you'll write the fucking check from your own fucking checkbook!"

And Ivory, himself, had his moments, too.

"Did you see the Sunday *Times*?" Seth Rubin, the film's still photographer, asked Jim on a Monday morning.

"No. What?"

"We had an article and a picture."

"Really? No, I haven't seen it. Was it good?"

"I just looked at the picture."

"Did you get credit?"

"Yes."

"Good. That's unusual. What was the picture?"

"The one on the Champs Elysees."

"Oh, no! You see? Never, *never* send stills to them! They're so *stupid! I'm* stupid for sending them! They'll unerringly go to the wrong still. Of all the things to choose from, all the good things, they pick a still of the *extras* on the Champs Elysees!"

And in the Nolte camp, Eric couldn't escape the breakdown of composure and restraint, either. Eventually, he became sour and abusively negative, skewering everyone on the stiletto of his magnificent wit. From his first words in the morning until he slipped into bed at night, he projected a sour outlook in expletives, threats and unprovoked attacks on everything that, for the moment, engaged his attention. Every innocent observation to him brought a snide response. Laudatory reactions to a gifted cellist's performance provoked the derisive title "Doctor Dave, Leader of the Kazoo Brigade."

And when he finally came to believe that the journal I was keeping and the verbatim notes of conversations would really find their way someday into a book like this, he quipped quickly, "You're so scared of your mediocrity, you're so terrified of your own anonymity, you think you have to make your presence known with verbal diarrhea in a futile search for immortality!"

His threats were equally wonderful: "I'm capable of such destruction, I'm warning all humanity—*your time is limited!*"

And: "Stay away from me or I'll twist off your nipples and use them as radio dials!"

The only time he smiled with genuine pleasure was when he was told, "Eric, you're so negative, you can't respond positively to anyone or anything on the face of this earth."

He liked that.

However, since Eric is fundamentally one of the gentlest and sweetest human beings one could ever hope to meet, all of his retorts were wrapped in an element of charm, which kept his demeanor from being resented and his words from sounding reprehensible. But the fact is, suffering under the heavy weight of Nick Nolte's increasingly demanding, irrational behavior and affected by the general madness that ultimately pervades every film project, Eric, too, succumbed to the pressures of production.

Now one might think that under these circumstances all parts of a motion picture would fly off in every direction, that all morale would collapse, and that everyone would lick wounds and curse the day he ever became involved with the film. More often than not, that *is* the case. But fortunately for Nick Nolte that wasn't the case with *Jefferson in Paris*. The saving grace for him was his deep respect for James Ivory. No matter how upset Nolte became with himself or with the failures he imagined or actually witnessed on the set, he never truly lost his faith in Ivory's directorial skills. It weakened from time to time, but it was never abandoned. And that's another fascinating aspect of Nick Nolte: once he believes in someone or something, only the most blatant evidence to the contrary can destroy that faith. James Ivory's calm, receptive manner never permitted the kind of provocation that could change Nolte's mind about the man.

In the face of growing tensions, Ivory continued to be open, to accept suggestions with equanimity in extremely difficult moments. For example, after nine unsuccessful and frustrating takes of a scene in which Jefferson is listening to the demands of French veterans who served in the American Revolution, someone other than the director offered an observation to one of the actors:

"It's not you. You're not getting it because the cue you're being given is wrong."

"What's wrong with it?"

"He's saying 'Yankee Doodle Dandy.' It should just be 'Yankee Doodle.' You're trying to sing 'Yankee Doodle Dandy went to town' when you should be singing 'Yankee Doodle went to town.' The rhythm is wrong. That's why you can't get it."

"But it's 'Yankee Doodle Dandy' in the script."

"The script is wrong."

"Jim, Jim, the cue should be 'Yankee Doodle,' not

'Yankee Doodle Dandy.'"

"No, it's 'Yankee Doodle Dandy.' Keep it that way."

Then the observer countered:

"'Yankee Doodle Dandy' was written by George M. Cohan in the 1920s, Jim. It wasn't the revolutionary song."

"Really? I didn't know that. That's wonderful. Okay, all right. Change the cue."

The next take became a print.

At another time:

John Trumbull was a promising young painter whom Jefferson had befriended and encouraged in the hope of developing American art. He lived at *de Langeac* with Jefferson while preparing one of his four epic paintings about the American Revolution. In the scene being filmed, he's working on a small canvas. Everything had been progressing well until someone addressed Ivory with, "Jim, the painting they're all gathered around is too small to be taken for the original."

"Why? What do you mean?"

"The one Trumbull did of Cornwallis's surrender at Yorktown is monumental in size. It's hanging in the rotunda of the Capitol building in Washington. The difference between what's hanging there and what Trumbull's doing here is going to look ridiculous to anybody who knows, and you'll be laughed out of the theaters for the mistake."

"Well, we can't do anything about it now."

"Why not give Trumbull a line explaining the difference?"

"That's a great idea!" Ivory agreed. "He can say it's a preliminary painting, something like a sketch in preparation for the real thing, which will be much larger."

He wrote a few lines and had them delivered to Trumbull.

The actor, Nigel Whitmey, was in heaven, and even Nolte felt an added sense of security in Ivory's quick action.

It's easy to assume that the gentleness with which Ivory accepted the correction is understandable in light of his not wanting to be attacked for a ridiculous error. However, another director under Ivory's pressure might have become exasperated by the discovery and raged at not having been informed of the mistake before the start of shooting.

It was this kind of equanimity that kept the growing madness from becoming totally unmanageable. This and the cleverness of Ismail Merchant.

Ismail encouraged and even participated in activities that would sustain the healthy bonds that had been developed in the early days of the schedule. He encouraged everyone to be in the film, if only as an extra. He even gave Eric a small role as a spy, and when Eric emerged from the makeup trailer in full costume, he glowed in the cheers of all who were waiting to see him.

Ismail knew, also, that daily lunches should become social events. It's difficult to be entirely bitter when tables are set on clean, colorful table-cloths, and plates, glasses and utensils aren't paper and plastic, when waiters serve everyone five course meals, when each table offers two bottles of wine, when desserts are intriguing pastries, when fruits and a variety of cheeses conclude every meal, and when any show of dissatisfaction brings a menu adjustment wherever possible to please the complainant. Though every meal wasn't entirely satisfactory to everyone, for the most part it was tasty and enjoyable. The lunches offered opportunities for relaxation and pleasant conversation. Laughter could always be heard ringing in the tents.

Unfortunately, Nolte seldom benefited directly from these daily gatherings because he preferred to remain in his dressing room. However, he benefited *in*directly because the daily lunches helped everyone else with whom Nick came in contact to keep a grip on increasingly unstable sensibilities.

And this kind of conviviality extended to partying, too. If for nothing else, *Jefferson in Paris* should have won some kind of award for the quality and number of its parties. After a Friday's call announcing the week's wrap, someone would inevitably host a special party at the schedule's location. It could be to celebrate an actor's completion of his or her contract. Or just a production crew's time-to-relax way of unwinding with friends. Or a gigantic birthday bash for Ivory, arranged with startling imagination by Ismail himself. Whatever the reason, parties flourished, and the sanguine nature of their intent acted, unquestionably, like emotional glue.

All of this helped, but unfortunately nothing can arrest Nolte's decline completely once he's in his spin. When anxieties have him spiraling, any intrusion, any demand made upon him will assume mountainous proportions. And since he hadn't completed his dubbing obligations for *I Love Trouble* at that time, these became a veritable Everest of difficulties for him.

The disturbing part about the dubbing wasn't the actual work. He was contractually committed to three days of work. And if Nick agrees to something with respect to his acting, he will honor that agreement with unwavering devotion. And it wasn't the work itself. Once he's in a studio, Nolte will invariably give himself fully to the task at hand. Rather, it was what he perceived to be an unwillingness on the part of the directors of *I Love Trouble* to inconvenience themselves and to accommodate him at a time when he was being weakened by the demands of the Jefferson role.

"I know Hollywood," he fumed. "Nobody in this business is willing to put himself out for anybody else. It's always a battle to get what you want. Look, there's a nine hour difference between here and LA, right? They want me to be in a studio here while they're in a studio there. But they're not willing to inconvenience themselves by getting up early in the morning to get to their studio. They want to sleep in and have a nice breakfast and take their goddamned time getting there. So with the nine hour difference, I'll have to get to *my* studio in the afternoon and then work for eight hours into the night. Well, fuck them. I want to start in the morning and be finished by the afternoon. They say they have a lot of problems and I should consider what they're going through; well, I have a lot of problems, too, and they should consider what *I'm* going through! They want me to adjust my schedule to satisfy them; well, let them adjust their schedule to satisfy *me*. Let them get out of bed a little earlier for three days. It won't kill 'em. They never bitch about waking up at three o'clock in the morning when they're on a set and have to shoot a scene. So there's nothing to bitch about now. They're just being goddamned selfish and unreasonable, that's all. So fuck 'em."

Of course, Nolte never said any of this directly to the directors of *I Love Trouble*. That was left to Eric and Nick's agent and his lawyer. Nolte channeled his energies, instead, into feeling beleaguered and abused. In this mat-

ter he was right. There was nothing to prevent the directors from acquiescing to his needs. And they knew it.
After many days of battling, Eric finally reported that the
dubbing would take place in the morning and that Nick
would be finished by late afternoon.

Nolte grinned. He was satisfied. He'd been vindicat-
ed. His understanding of how things worked in the
industry had been validated.

"They should have agreed in the first place," he snorted. "We didn't have to go through all this shit. And I did-
n't have to have more of my energies drained unnecessarily."

Despite the distress he'd experienced, though, he
spent three full days in a little French studio tediously
dubbing scenes, without a single complaint. And the
open telephone line between Paris and Los Angeles crack-
led only with laughter and friendliness—as if the heated
disagreement had never taken place.

Eight

Everyone knows how costly motion picture production can be. The average budget of a major feature film today is in the neighborhood of sixty million dollars. This has far-reaching significance. Not only in respect to the development of production values, but in respect to the perversion of human values. Since every day's work can cost hundreds of thousands of dollars, everything must be done to see that work continues. Natural disasters can't be controlled, of course. But man-made mistakes are avoidable.

In motion picture production, the biggest mistake that can be made is one that upsets the film's star. Why? Because an upset star may charge off the set, lock himself or herself in a dressing room and refuse to come out for hours. And lost hours will mean lost money. Hundreds of thousands of budget dollars wasted for nothing, jeopardizing the entire endeavor. Consequently, film actors are babied and pampered shamelessly. And more than that, they are feared. Every whim is considered, every demand is satisfied. Do you want another car? All right, you may have another car. Do you want a larger dressing room? Certainly, we can find a larger dressing room. You need a couch to rest on? Of course—Katherine, get two assistants and bring a couch out here for him, will you? Pillows, too? Absolutely—Katherine, don't forget some pillows.

When we add the public's celebrity-loving mentality to this kind of treatment, we get the creation of a pseudo-royalty. A group of people that assumes royal airs, though it rarely sees itself as doing so. The group is not limited to actors. Directors fit into it as well.

Of course, Nolte accepts everyone in the film-making business as part of this royalty as long as that person seems to be outside the mainstream and has made some kind of mark for himself. Sean Penn is definitely in the group. Harrison Ford is not. Oliver Stone is in the group. Martin Scorsese is sitting high on a throne. John Travolta and Nicolas Cage used to be in the group, but they've become studio icons now, and they've blemished their independent spirits with commercial tripe. Terry Gilliam is royalty and Billy Friedkin, too. And, certainly, Nick fits squarely in the center of the group. However, he rationalizes his royal behavior, his aloofness, his insulation, his impatience, his demanding personality, his benign neglect of associates, his moodiness, and his control of people and situations. He sees himself as a free, democratic individual in a position of artistic importance, beleaguered by fans, pressured by demands and justifiably "requesting" the freedom to create.

He's not to be faulted for this, though. Like all stars, he's been forced to feel royal and autocratic by what is euphemistically called "Star Treatment," but which, in reality, is the corrupting deference that every royal personage believes is his natural right.

When he's at home, between films and away from public recognition, Nolte can drop most of his regal attitudes. He can joke endlessly with acquaintances. He can share his deepest thoughts and feelings. He can enjoy the company of others. But when "His Highness" is on a set working, when he's feeling the strain of his responsibilities, he reverts automatically to the royal habits he's now developed, and he becomes someone who likes to have others near but, like aristocracy, only when their presence or their help is required.

When he's made aware of this behavior, he explains it with "It's not a conscious thing. It's the result of being on this emotional roller coaster so long. I withdraw. I become negative and confrontational. But then that's good. Confrontation stimulates me again, and I can go out and do a little more work."

Nevertheless, because royalty loves royalty, Nick will *always* welcome the company of other industry aristocrats without negativism or confrontation. When Billy Friedkin came to Paris on vacation, Nolte welcomed him eagerly and happily, despite the fact that he was always tired and stressed-out.

Billy stayed at the Ritz Hotel, too, on the first floor in what is called the Marcel Proust Suite. He is a Proust fanatic. He's read all of Proust and practically everything about him. He was in Paris, visiting Marcel Proust historical sites.

He appeared at the door of Nick's suite when we had returned late from the day's work at the *de Langeac* set. Nick's greeting pulled him into the room with a handshake for a warm embrace, and he was invited to stay for dinner. Room service brought them filet of trout as only the Ritz Hotel can prepare it. They dined slowly and gabbed pleasantly until midnight.

Billy Friedkin is an entertaining raconteur. He has a

natural sense of timing and the ability to take an ordinary situation and turn it into something vivid and exciting. And when he's thrilled by something like a Marcel Proust experience, his narrative can light up a room. It did that night.

As tired as he was supposed to be, Nolte reveled in Friedkin's presence and his story.

"I went to Proust's elementary school yesterday and I asked, 'You wouldn't by any chance keep records from that far back, would you?'"

"'*Oui, Monsieur.*'"

"'You mean you still have Marcel Proust's school records?!'"

"'*Oui, Monsieur.*'"

"'Oh, my God, that's incredible! Would it be possible to see them?'"

"'*Oui, Monsieur*, but it will be necessary to locate them first.'"

"He took me into an old, musty room where records were stacked on tables, shelves, the floor—everywhere. The search began. Dust flew every time something was moved. But eventually, there they were—we found the actual records of Marcel Proust! And you know what he failed as a kid? French! Can you believe it? This guy, who wrote one of the greatest fucking books ever written in French—maybe the greatest book ever written in *any* language—this fucking guy failed *French!*"

We laughed at the absurd incongruity.

"That's great, that's really great!" Nick said. "Sounds like you had a terrific day."

"Oh, the best, the best. I made copies of those records. Hey, I've got 'em now. They're mine!"

Then, just as animatedly, Nolte described the

Jefferson shoot. He talked about locations, what he'd seen and enjoyed, how the work was going, his acting, Merchant and Ivory, and their next project, which would be about Pablo Picasso and, possibly, star Al Pacino as Picasso.

"Al? Picasso?" Billy said. "Al can't play Picasso. Picasso was bald. Al can't act without his hair, for Chrissake. He's like Samson. Take his fucking hair away and he's dead!"

"The hair is his look?" Nick said.

"Fuck, yes! The hair's his look and the look is Al. Take the look away and you've got nothing! I directed Al in *Cruisin'*. I know. Al got this idea that he should get a gay haircut. Y'know, he's playin' an undercover cop inside the gay hangouts. So, he went to a gay barber, and the guy cut him just the way the guys were wearing their hair at that time—slicked back, short, y'know. Then Al comes on the set and says, 'Billy, look what they did to me.' I took one look and almost died. He looked terrible! I had to shut down the whole production."

"You shut it down?"

"Shit, yes. Two months. Had to wait for the fucking hair to grow back in. Al can't play Picasso. Picasso was bald."

The next day, because he'd enjoyed Friedkin's visit so much, Nolte went to the Picasso museum with him. They walked around for hours, and when they emerged into the sunlight again, Billy grunted and said, "Pacino could play the ass off that role. He's Picasso. I didn't think so because of that hair business, but when I saw those photos of Picasso—shit, man, hair or no hair, Pacino would be great!"

At another time, Terry Gilliam called to say he need-ed a meeting with Nick to talk about his participation in a project that was close to Gilliam's heart. Now, ordinarily, discussion about a new film while he's suffering with a present assignment would have been unthinkable. But this was Terry Gilliam and, in the Nolte reference, not some schlock director. A meeting was arranged. Terry came to the hotel. He, Nick and Eric locked themselves in Nick's suite for more than an hour. After he'd left, Nick and Eric came into my room.

"Isn't he terrific?" Nolte said with unusual enthusiasm.

"He's great," Eric agreed.

"The energy that man has! Man, he's something!"

"I loved the way he pitched the film."

"Yeah. And I like the title, too: *The Defective Detective*. It's great!"

"Are you going to take it on?" I asked.

"I'm thinking about it. It sounds interesting, and it's something he's dying to do. I think I'd like to work with him."

"He's on fire?"

"He's burning."

Friedkin and Gilliam had been Visiting Royalty, and for contact with most of the industry's royalty Nick Nolte will always put aside his complaints and find the necessary time. The next day, though, Nolte switched right back into his work mode, focusing intently and singularly on a difficult, upcoming scene.

"Let's talk about Sally for a while."

Every good screenplay has relationships that compel an actor to walk that fine and delicate line between the sublime and the ridiculous. While in Paris, Thomas Jefferson's loves were more complex than a simple Eternal

Triangle. They were more like an Impossible Quadrangle. Besides his passionate love for Maria Cosway and his deep, possessive love for his daughter Patsy, Jefferson's feelings for his fifteen-year-old slave Sally Hemings, added so much uncertainty to his life that it's easy to understand why he longed for the order and serenity of Monticello.

Until recent DNA findings, which identify Thomas Jefferson as the father of at least one of Sally Heming's children, historians had been loathe to admit to this master-slave affair. They argued that the purity of Jefferson's moral character precluded the possibility of anything ever having happened between them. Blinded by their desire to protect an icon, scholars continually sidestep the sexual proclivities of great leaders.

In *Jefferson in Paris*, Nolte had to face the complexities of this relationship head-on.

"Do you think I love Sally?"

"In a way, yes," I answered.

"So do I."

"You have to love her, but there's also lust in there."

"Okay. So why do I love her? Because she's Monticello to me, too, that's why."

"Good. Everything about the Monticello Ideal is woven into your being. Your heart is in Monticello, and if Sally is part of Monticello, your heart is in her, too."

"But she's my slave so I can't be open and public about it."

"You wouldn't want to be even if she weren't your slave. Sally may be nice, but she's beneath your station in every respect—culturally, intellectually, educationally. There's nothing there that would make you want a public life with her even if she were white."

"So what I'm feeling for her is the warm love of a

benevolent master who identifies her with home and all the good things of my life back there."

"Right. And there's lust, not the passion of deep love. Don't forget, Maria and you have just split up. That's where the passion was. Sally's just young, pretty, juicy and available."

"Okay. Now let's put Patsy into this," he added.

"Patsy's the other part of the Monticello Ideal. She's really the heart of it. And she knows this."

"Because I've promised her that she'll be Monticello's mistress when we get back to Virginia. So when she discovers that Sally and I are making it in the sack together, she's jealous—"

"Very jealous. Your daughter feels an almost incestuous love for you—"

"So she's resentful towards me and Sally, and she's afraid that I've forgotten the covenant I made with her."

"Exactly."

"And I'm caught in the middle. I'm not going to give up Sally because she's my connection with home in the gentlest, most satisfying and undemanding way that's possible in France."

"And you can't allow the daughter you love so deeply to suffer the way she's suffering."

"This is an emotional nightmare for me."

"Right. You never forget that Sally's not only *your* slave. Patsy's the Mistress of Monticello, so Sally's *her* slave, too, and here's her slave threatening everything that's meaningful in her life. Now, how can you convey your love for Patsy without giving up Sally and, at the same time, not seem like a liar and a fraud?"

"This one's gonna be a bitch."

And it was. But Nolte's careful preparation allowed

him to avoid looking like a lecherous old fool with Sally, and an indifferent, cold father with Patsy.

In time, almost everyone in a production has some kind of physical breakdown. Colds. Flu. *Some*thing. When my turn came, it was a brutal cold that lasted three days. I lay in my bed snuffling, wheezing and coughing. The doors to Eric's room and Nick's suite were open at all times and Nolte walked in and out like a mothering hen, constantly checking on my condition and clucking happily at my misery.

Eric barged in. He'd been downstairs in the hotel's fitness center.

Nick came in from his suite.

"Where've you been?" he asked Eric.

"In the gym, working out."

"You're always working out. Every time I need you, you're working out."

"Jeez. I workout only in the evenings. Hey, that good-looking girl was there again."

"What happened?" I asked.

"She told me she's enjoying herself. I asked, 'With your boyfriend?' and she said, 'Oh, he's not my boyfriend. He's nice, but I don't think of him that way. I can do things without him.'"

"That was your cue," I said.

"I know."

"Did you pick up on it?"

"I didn't say anything."

"Why *not*?"

"I don't know. I just hung my head. I didn't know what to say."

"You should have asked her to dinner. Say you're going out with some actor friends and you'd like her to join you. She'd have jumped at it."

"Is that all you guys do?" Nolte asked. "Enjoy yourselves while I work like a dog all by myself?"

"But you get all the attention of the star, and what do we get, huh?" Eric shot back with a grin.

"That's all you guys do—go out eating, drinking, wearing yourselves down on me. *That's* why you got sick, Mel—guilt!"

"I like the total absence of compassion in you. It has the purity of totalitarianism. You've arrived. You're a pure *Nazi!*"

"I'm going back to my room. You stay in your hospital ward and you, Eric, you go out and eat and drink and come in at all hours smelling up the room like a brewery and never thinking of me and how I'm all alone, working and obsessing—"

"Nazi Nick, go back to your den. I'm suffering too much for this."

"Good. You have to learn to be like me and suffer for your art. Here's an article in this magazine about Sam Peckinpah. (He threw an issue of *Film Comment* on my bed.) You guys should read it. *There* was a man who knew how to suffer! Did he go out drinking and getting sick like you? Not when he was making *The Wild Bunch.* He didn't touch a drop. He stayed healthy. And why? Because he knew discipline! He was willing to suffer for his art. There's a lesson in that for you guys!"

"Like when you were making *48 Hours,*" Eric said, laughing. "You boozed every night!"

"That wasn't boozing. That was work! The character was a drinker. I was working to stay in character. You think I liked all that drinking? You think I was enjoying myself? That was work! I was suffering for my art. That's what you guys have to learn to do—not enjoy yourselves and get sick from guilt!"

"Go back to your room, Nazi Nick."

"I am...I am...I'm going back to suffer...I think I'll call downstairs and arrange to get a nice massage."

"Some suffering!"

"All for art, all for art. Are you going to be all right, Mister Death?"

"I'll be fine, Nazi Nick."

"Okay. See you later, Mister Death."

"See you later, Nazi Nick."

The next day, he came into my room and lectured like a parent.

"If you wouldn't stay out so late, you wouldn't be getting sick. What time did you come in the other night? You're not taking care of yourself, and you're not going to make it through the film if you don't take care of yourself."

"Yes, Mother."

"I mean it, your body can't take this night life the way it did when you were a kid."

No matter what distress he's experiencing personally, off the set and away from the camera Nolte can still rally in certain moments with pain-relieving humor and heart-warming concern.

This is true even when his own health suffers and he's the one in physical pain. *I Love Trouble* produced Premature Ventricular Contractions, the infamous heart irregularities; *Jefferson in Paris* gave him boils, piles and anal lesions.

"Squeeze this boil on my back for me, will you? It's killing me. I can't even get a shirt on."

"Let's get a doctor on this."

"No. Squeeze it."

"It's gonna hurt."

"Don't worry about that. Just break that mother and get it all out."

"Okay, Nicholas. Hold on to something."

The squeezing was horrendous but eventually the boil popped and a gallon of pus and blood squirted all over the room and down his back.

"There, that should do it."

"Ooooohh—better—much, much better—*great!* I'd thank you but I'm not sure you deserve it. You almost killed me."

He recovered quickly from the boil problem, but the anal lesions were another matter. The pain was more than he could bear. He loved to display his tortured posterior to Eric and me. He'd barge into our rooms naked and bend over, saying, "Look at this thing, will ya? What the hell is it? What do you see?"

And I would chant, "Massa's ass is very sad. Massa's ass is very bad. Massa's got a sad, bad ass—Bad-Ass Massa!"

For days, he suffered terribly. He sat in a tub of hot water and groaned from the pain. When that didn't help, he used cold water. That brought some measure of relief but it was only temporary and short-lived. He tried to get through the nights with ice packs and even an ice-filled wine bottle jammed against the crack of his buttocks. But they usually fell off or rolled away the moment he fell asleep. Nothing allowed the lesions to heal. The skin became leathery, grotesquely swollen, purple in color.

"It's not getting any better, is it?" he asked, staring at his problem, with his head between his spread legs and his naked butt facing the full-length mirror in my room.

"Well, that depends. A love-sick baboon might think it's becoming more exciting every day."

"What should I do?"

"Find a baboon."

"Don't fool around. I'm serious. What should I do?"

"What d'ya mean, what should I do? See a doctor, for Chrissake. You should have seen one days ago."

"Yeah."

It had become so bad, he was unable to act. James Ivory had to work around him for three days. He needed medical attention desperately. Someone in the Merchant Ivory company recommended a French quack whose office looked like a hangout for the homeless. Papers, magazines and dirty clothes were strewn everywhere except on the "cat's armchair" which was a filthy, clawed wreck reserved exclusively for the "doctor's" feline friend. The examination and diagnosis could have been the work of a demented witch doctor. They did absolutely nothing to help Nick with his problem. He suffered magnificently, though, telling everyone who would listen about the agony he was enduring and the fascinating appearance of his ass.

Fortunately, two real doctors who happened to be staying at the hotel were willing to come to his suite when they were called. Their examination was thorough; their diagnosis made sense. The lesions were the result of excessive lymph gland secretions, a disorder often brought on by extreme stress. Antibiotics, surgical soap and some kind of healing paste were prescribed and obtained. And the very next day, Nolte was able to walk again, with a miraculous fifty-percent improvement in his condition.

One of the more interesting aspects of this experience was Nolte's sense of helplessness. He had not only been physically incapacitated by his lesions, he had been confused and disoriented by them, as well. "What should I do?" he'd asked innocently. And that question reflects Nick's strong reliance upon others to help him in his moments of distress. That "others" has, in the main, been his nephew and principal assistant, Eric. What's especially fascinating is that Nolte has never fully appreciated how important Eric had become to him, nor has he realized to this day how complete reliance upon an assistant can make one uncertain about simple problem solving by oneself.

"Eric," Nick shouted one night as he charged through my room to get to Eric's room, "my phones are out. What am I going to do?"

"Don't worry," Eric responded, "I'll take care of it."

Eric reported the telephone failure to the front desk.

"What'd they say?"

"They said, 'We're switching switchboards and some telephones have been affected. We'll look into Mister Nolte's telephones immediately and correct the failure.'"

"Oh, good."

Five minutes later:

"What the fuck—! My phones are *still* out! What am I going to do? Where's Eric?"

"He left for dinner with Lisa."

"What am I going to do?"

"They said they'd fix it."

"I know, but they haven't done it."

"Then call them again on my phone."

"Oh...yeah...."

He made the call himself.

"This is Mister Nolte. I called earlier to report my phones not working...I know, but I have a conference call I have to make to America...Thank you."

He replaced the receiver. There was no look of satisfaction, no sense of relief. Only a troubled, frustrated frown as he shuffled back into his room.

Eric had not been there to take care of the matter for him.

While he can be unbearable at times to his assistant, Nolte never loses his warmth and his gentleness with production personnel to whom he has become especially attached. Working every day with his makeup artists, Nick invariably develops a wonderful rapport that transcends the usual actor-helper relationship. Makeup calls, as everyone knows, are scheduled mostly in the morning. It's a quiet time. A time of intimacy between the specialist and the actor, a time when the star can relax and place himself entirely in the expert hands of another person. Gentle joking takes place. Experiences are exchanged. Little secrets are revealed. And though he groans about having to wake up early for his makeup calls, Nick always settles into them with a charming sense of pleasure. In the wee hours of the morning, sequestered with the makeup artists, Nolte is usually at his very best.

Pauline and Betty were especially delightful people, conscientious in the extreme. They took their assignment so seriously, even the emotional condition of their subject became a matter of personal concern. They worried about anything in their work that might upset him, not only because they disliked unpleasantness, but because they genuinely liked him. And Nolte enjoyed them even more than they enjoyed him.

As we arrived on the set one morning, Nick was surprised to find Pauline waiting for him outside his trailer.

After sending Stanislas for his second breakfast of bacon and eggs, he turned toward her.

She was obviously troubled.

"What's the matter?" he asked.

"Betty and I have been refused the makeup bus this morning," she explained.

Nolte was surprised. This was definitely not the way the star of a film should be treated. "Why?" he asked. "What happened?"

"That bitch hairdresser has taken over the bus. She wants it for Greta and some extras."

"What do you mean?"

"Betty and I can't use it. They've taken it away. Do you mind if we do you in your trailer?"

Nolte saw her distress. He smiled gently. "No. That's fine."

There was an audible sigh of relief. Nick grinned and embraced her warmly.

Betty came out of the trailer at that moment, her eyes puffed and red. She'd been crying.

"Good morning, Betty," Nolte greeted her gently. "How are you?"

"Not too good. Good morning. We've been trying to get this sorted out."

"Now it's sorted, right?"

"Is it?"

"Nick doesn't mind," Pauline informed her partner.

"I'll be inside," Nick said and he disappeared into his trailer.

Everyone was grinning.

"He took that well," Pauline murmured.

"Yes, he did," I agreed. "But you had nothing to be concerned about. He'll do more for you than he will for me."

"That's nice," Pauline said.

"He likes you and Betty very much."

"That's *very* nice."

"It's also true."

"That makes me very happy."

There's something extremely captivating about Nick. It's an innate goodness. Despite his craziness, despite his extreme narcissism, he's the kind of person who really doesn't want to hurt another living soul. And given the chance just to be himself, he will affect others wonderfully with his basic gentleness.

However, his development hasn't reached the point yet of thinking about *helping* others. Not in any way that I have personally seen. Oh, he'll rarely pass a homeless person without dropping some bills into his or her hand. And I'm certain he gives to particular charities. But he won't extend himself to *offering* help if that will impinge upon his time and his energies. Not, at least, to anyone or anything that I'm aware of. Instead, when he's asked to do something for another person who is not directly related to his life or his interests, he hesitates. He can't seem to derive pleasure from initiating action that will make others happy. In his mind, that approach to happiness may be an encroachment upon his personal independence.

"Let's go for a walk, okay?" he suggested.

"Sounds good."

"A short one. Twenty minutes. I've got to get out for a while."

On the walk, I said, "There's something I'd like you to do."

As soon as the words were out, I detected that familiar coolness in his manner.

"Stanislas and I were talking a couple of days ago," I

persisted. "I asked him what he planned to do when the picture ends and we go home. He made a face and shrugged. Said he'll probably go back to Normandy. He has to take care of his baby. I asked if he could get another job. He said no, that it was almost impossible. He's qualified to be a 2nd AD, but in France *any* job on a film is almost impossible to get unless you know someone."

"Well, that's the same everywhere," Nolte cut in.

"But he's going to need work and he'll go anywhere for it."

"There's nothing—"

"I don't mean the States. That's not the point, though. Let me finish."

"Okay, go ahead."

"Someone asked me about you. 'How's Nick? Is everything all right? Is there anything he needs?' I told him everything's as good as can be. Then he asked, 'Is his driver all right?' So, I told him how pleased you are with Stanislas."

"Yeah."

"I gave him a good buildup. Always on time, thoroughly dependable, never complains, gives above-and-beyond. You know."

"Yeah."

"Then I said, 'If you can use him again it'd be great. Good for Merchant Ivory and good for him.' And he said, 'Absolutely.' Well, yesterday I told Stanislas to follow up on this. He's going to. Now, if you'll say something to Ismail, too, that kind of reinforcement will probably get him a job—or at the very least make him stick in their minds until an opening comes along. Will you do it?"

"I don't know about that," Nolte answered. "I don't know."

Eventually, he did say something in his driver's behalf, but he probably would never have helped if he hadn't been urged to do so by someone else. And the fact that he had to change his mind indicates that his initial reaction, in that moment, had little in it to show compassion for, and interest in, Stanislas's predicament. Nolte is not a heartless person, though. Far from it. It just takes a little time for him to come around, and when he does, he usually believes it was his idea in the first place.

Nine

The days were racing by. The end was drawing near. Eric and I suggested to Nick that, like other members of the production, he should sponsor and pay for a little production party at the close of a week's work.

"No."

"It would be nice," Eric said. "Almost everybody's done it. Even Jim Ivory."

"I don't want to. If *you* want to do it, go ahead."

"You want everybody to call you Mister Cheapo, right?" I asked.

"I don't give a fuck what they call me."

Eric and I smiled at each other. Later, we decided to give the party ourselves.

"I've been thinking about that party," Nick told me. "I don't think you and Eric should do it."

"Why not?"

"It'll make me look bad."

"Then give it yourself."

"No." And he was adamant.

As it happened, Vicki came to Paris for a weekend on her second, Merchant Ivory authorized Concorde flight. When she heard about the party disagreement, she raised her eyebrows and shook her head in disbelief.

Eric and I never learned what was actually said between her and Nick about the subject, but Nolte approached us somewhat shamefacedly the next morning and said, "I've changed my mind."

"About what?"

"The party. I think it might be a good idea. These people have been very nice to me. A party will show I appreciate what they've done. Let's make it a good one."

And later, he reached into the money shelf in his room, pulled out enough francs to finance a royal ball, and handed them to Eric and me with a boyish grin.

I caught Vicki's eye. She was smiling wisely and nodding her lovely head.

Next to the final cast celebration thrown by Ismail Merchant, the Nolte wrap party turned out to be the biggest, best-catered, booziest bash of the entire shoot. Everyone was happy. Everyone was complimentary. And Nick took the laudatory comments like a Prince of the People—graciously, smilingly, appreciatively—as if throwing that party was something he'd been planning to do from the first day of his arrival in France.

As part of his general playfulness, Nolte loves to showboat. He'll do it even during periods of distress. Somehow, he'll come alive when an opportunity to "play it big" comes along. He'll grab hold of a harmless situation and run happily with it as long as it will confound and unbalance the opposing participants. It doesn't take much to get him started either. It's all a lovely game. And it doesn't matter too much if he wins the game or loses it. In these times, he's more delighted by playing than he is interested in outcome.

The end of *Jefferson in Paris* was approaching rapidly.

Everyone began to talk about what he or she intended to do next. Everyone, that is, except Nick, whose reaction to any suggestion that the final wrap was in sight bordered on the violent.

"It's almost over, Nick," I remarked.

"Jesus, don't say that! Never say that!"

"Why not?"

"Because it's never over until it's over, and talking about it only makes it worse!"

"Is this more of your craziness?"

"No. It's the way it is. There's so much to do yet, we can't start to think of it being over. Think that way and we let down. We become unfocused, and we lose the picture in the final weeks. Never, *never* talk about it being almost over!"

He was right. Things could still go wrong. And when they do at this stage of production, Nolte can become almost pathologically frantic. Of course, things did go wrong.

Besides some smaller, intimate moments, two major scenes remained to be filmed by Nick. And they would require every ounce of energy and every pinpoint of concentration he and his fellow actors would be able to pull from themselves.

Though Thomas Jefferson had countless ministerial duties, he always found time for art and artists. Art fed his soul. It was the only area in which he admitted American inferiority to Europe. He longed for American art to rise to the level of excellence that he was experiencing in Paris. There, galleries attracted the outstanding painters and sculptors of the day.

The greatest sculptor of the age was Jean Antoine Houdon. Jefferson never lost an opportunity to view his work.

One of the two remaining scenes for Nick had Jefferson and Maria Cosway meeting in Houdon's studio. The location for this scene was a school, the *Maison d'Education de la Légion d'Honneur* in *St. Denis*, where one of the huge rooms was transformed amazingly into Houdon's studio. Sculptures in various stages of development and all the exotic equipment of this genius filled the room. It was an astounding duplication of an eighteenth century sculptor's workshop. And with over eighty costumed principals and extras wandering about, the effect was another startling moment of time travel.

It would have been wonderful if the day's work had gone as well as the set appeared. But it didn't.

This time the problem wasn't twentieth century street noises or airplane engines. This time, the difficulty was internal.

Nolte had determined the arc of the scene. It would go from puzzlement in light comedy to certainty about moral values. It would show Jefferson delightfully confused, and humanized by the confusion. The problem with this was that Greta Schacci had not made the same determination. This, unfortunately, was one scene that Greta and Nick hadn't discussed in advance, one upon which they hadn't reached agreement. The absence of agreement caused divergent and conflicting interpretations.

James Ivory found himself with two actors almost totally out-of-sync and no clear picture of his own to communicate to them. This time, Ivory's unwillingness to give his actors interpretive direction produced the worst kind of results. Since Ivory works out a scene's blocking slowly for visual effect, since camera angles are determined on the basis of actor movement, and since Ivory accepts input so readily, Greta's and Nick's suggestions now created confusion. Greta's came from an extremely sensitive feeling for motion, not from a desire to achieve a clearly delineated scene objective; Nick's came from a desire to achieve a clearly delineated scene objective and not from a subjective feel for movement. As a result, camera angles based upon their actions became forced and troublesome. And everyone wasted huge chunks of time and energy trying to solve each new problem.

Ivory, feeling his control slipping away, pulled his actors together for a whispered conference. What was said in that huddle remains unknown; however, both Greta and Nick focused intently upon him, and when they returned to their places they seemed to wait more patiently for his suggestions.

Eventually, blocking and camera difficulties were resolved to Ivory's satisfaction. But Greta and Nick remained uncertain about achieving their respective designs. They'd still have to work them out by themselves.

It may have been this bad start that upset matters or it may have been just a jinxed morning but things did not improve. Actually they got worse. When the camera did roll finally, numerous takes were required to catch the simplest moments.

An example:

Jefferson had informed Maria that he couldn't return to America without the consent of Congress. The script gave Maria a simple response: "So, you are waiting for permission."

After numerous takes on that one sentence, James Ivory was ready to pull out his hair. No matter what he said, the line delivery failed to satisfy him.

"No, Greta," he would say softly in a number of ways, "try to say it a little faster. You're drawing it out too much."

It was clear that Greta was becoming increasingly frustrated; it was equally clear that Nolte was chewing himself into a frenzy.

Eventually, the take was accepted but not before patience had been stretched to the breaking point, and not before an enormous amount of time had been expended unnecessarily.

And what had been the problem? Greta's inability to deliver a line? Certainly not. Greta Scacchi is a gifted actor, capable of creating wonderfully sensitive character-izations. The problem had been James Ivory himself, and one little word. Instead of saying the line as it had been written, Greta had inadvertently made a contraction of "you are" into "you're." The line she repeated constantly to Ivory's dissatisfaction became: "So, you're waiting for permission." And that contraction caused her to draw out the word "so" and to emphasize the word "permission." The delivery became "Soooo, you're waiting for per*mis*sion." And the unwritten subtext became "I see. *That's* why you're not going home now. I didn't know that."

The sentence as it was written in the script, with no contraction, compelled the faster delivery that Ivory wanted. "So, you *are* waiting for permission." The sub-text then would become "I suspected that all along." This would have created a challenge on Maria's part, a chal-lenge that Greta would have been forced to deliver faster.

One little word. Numerous takes. Shortened tempers. And valuable time lost.

Now, the question becomes: Why did Ivory need so many takes? Why didn't he bring the problem's solution to Greta's attention immediately? Who can say? It may have been directorial weakness. But more likely, it was the extraordinary pressures of the final days; they may have reached even James Ivory and dulled his usual awareness.

Whatever the reason, filming the Houdon scene was an ordeal—one that threw Nolte and everyone else into another tailspin—one that gave substance to his Yogi Berra cry, "Never say it's almost over! It's *never* over until it's over!"

Difficulties like the Houdon scene had unhinged the *Jefferson* schedule badly. And, though it had been a five-day-week shoot, it became necessary for Nick and some of the others to work on a Saturday. Some people were asked if they would work; others were told they would have to work. Those who were asked said they'd rather not; those who were told said they were offended that they hadn't been asked. No one was happy. The approach had been a tactical error by Ismail Merchant.

Nolte, of course, was asked, not told. And being asked, he declined.

Production Manager Humbert Balsan apologized: it was unfortunate; everyone knew how much Nick needed his weekends off; Ismail was truly sorry, but it couldn't be helped; and Ismail hoped Nick would understand and, please, forgive what was unavoidable.

"Why don't we just extend the schedule another day?" Nolte asked.

"That's not possible. We can't," Balsan explained.

"Why not?"

"There are reasons. Location reasons. Banking reasons."

"I don't get it," Nick pressed him. "It won't cost any more to extend the schedule another day than it will to shoot an extra day on Saturday."

"I can't explain it. But believe me, if it were possible, we'd do it. Please understand, Nick."

What Nolte "understood" was that he was being told a lie. "It's not locations or financing," he told Pauline and Betty as they applied his makeup. "It's Thandie."

Thandie Newton, who played Sally Hemings, Jefferson's young slave-paramour, had received three film offers, with shooting to start on the first of the pictures the day after *Jefferson*'s final wrap. She had told everyone of her good fortune, and everyone was happy for her.

"Yeah, I think it's Thandie—and if it *is* Thandie, then they're lying to us. Look at it this way: we need another day of shooting, she has to start her next film on Monday, Ismail wants to accommodate her. So instead of extending our schedule one day and having us work on Monday, he helps her out by making it Saturday."

"That makes sense," Pauline agreed. "Oh, well…if it's to help Thandie…"

"That's not the point," Nick said. "They lied to us."

"Why would they do that?"

"Because they're scared. They think accommodating Thandie this way could look like favoritism, some kind of special consideration, and they're afraid that would upset everyone else."

"That's silly."

"They're not thinking. She wouldn't lose her film if she couldn't get there until Tuesday. Disney's gonna be distributing it. I know those guys. That's just a game they play. They love to get their own way. Ismail could keep her through Monday and she wouldn't lose her picture."

He looked almost gleeful. Ismail was playing with them. The game was on!

"Y'know, when I was doing *Grace Quigley* with Katharine Hepburn, she wanted a day off. Golan and Globus were the producers. They couldn't see it. So she bought it from them."

Pauline was astounded. "*Bought* it?"

"That's right."

And here Nolte went into one of his remarkable imitations of Katharine Hepburn.

"She said, 'I want that day off. I'll pay for it. Nick and I will split what it costs, won't we Nick?' And I said, 'Sure, that's okay with me.' So we bought the day off. Later, I said to her, 'What's it going to cost to buy that day?' And she said, 'Oh, not much; maybe fifty thousand. Twenty-five each.' And I said, 'Do me a favor Katy, don't ever volunteer me again.' But maybe that's what I ought to be doing here."

"Would you do that?" Pauline asked in fascination.

"Sure I would. What the hell, just tell 'em to keep my last check. It'd be worth twenty-five, thirty thousand to me. I'm going to tell Ismail and Humbert. What d'ya think they'll say?"

He was enjoying himself immensely.

"They wouldn't know how to deal with it," I guessed. "They'd probably laugh at first and believe you were joking. Then when they'd see you're serious, they'd get very nervous."

"You think they'd do it?"

"No. But it's worth a try if you don't mind spending that kind of money."

"How much could it cost?"

"What's the matter, you getting nervous?"

"No. But it couldn't cost more than fifty thousand, could it?"

"I wouldn't have the faintest idea."

"I'm gonna do it! It'll be fun just to see how they react."

Later that day, Nick met Humbert Balsan and made his offer.

The production manager reacted with surprise and embarrassment.

"Really? Well…I…I don't know…I'll…I'll tell Ismail."

When he saw Nick again, Balsan conveyed Ismail's answer.

"I'm sorry, Nick. We can't do that," he said.

"Why not?" Nolte was smiling at Humbert's discomfort.

"There are a lot of reasons."

"Like what?"

"I can't really explain them."

The vagueness of the response convinced Nick that the real reason was, as he had suspected all along, Thandie's new film commitment.

"Y'know what we ought to do now?" he said eagerly to me. "We ought to write something. Will you do it? Y'know, something like a parody of Jefferson's response when he was brought up on charges in Virginia. Make it funny. Get everything Ismail's done, all his foul-ups, into it. Will you do it?"

"No."

He seemed crushed. "Why not?"

"Because you've already made your point. A letter like that, even if it's a parody, would seem like you're complaining. You've had your fun. Anything more would be overkill. Move on."

He thought about that. Then he nodded his head in agreement. "But I nailed them, didn't I?"

Would he have bought the day if Ismail had agreed? Yes, I believe he would have. And would the price have bothered him? Not one bit. It would all have been a brilliant victory, another excellent story to tell on future shoots. However, he didn't feel he'd lost anything by Ismail's refusal, either. Ismail had won this one; Nick had to work on Saturday. But he'd enjoyed the little game. He'd confounded and unbalanced the producer. What's more, he'd made a lasting impression on Pauline and Betty with his imaginative showboating. For a day or so, he was a happy man.

Every film has scenes that are shot without sound. Later, the lines are dubbed in over the action. With James Ivory, temporary dubbing takes place on a tape recorder before the final sound is done in a studio. Nick was handed a few pages of speeches to be dubbed. The prospect rattled him.

Eric told me that Nolte was in another of his fits and that he needed me.

I found him in the makeup room.

"Help me with these goddamned voice-overs," he growled. "I'll read them, you listen."

Some of his words were mispronounced; he took the corrections quietly. But when he had difficulty with a particular sentence, he snapped, "I can't do this! It's written wrong. This needs a period here instead of a comma!"

"A period is different from a comma—"

"I know that. But—Jesus, why do you always have to oppose me?!"

"A period will give you a different read."

"Don't...don't...don't give me a grammar lesson. I don't need a grammar lesson now!"

I grinned at him.

"Now, you've ruined my train of thought. All I said was I'm going to use a period instead of a comma and you have to make an issue of it. I ask for your help and I get a grammar lesson. Read the line for me. Read it, go ahead, I wanna hear you read it."

I read the line, using the comma.

"That's what I need," he grumbled. "I need that pause."

"That's what a comma does; it separates things."

"A period does the same thing."

"No it doesn't."

"All right, all right, it doesn't. You know what the problem really is? I hate doing voice-overs without a lot of rehearsals. Streisand rehearsed them over and over until I knew exactly what I was saying."

"This is only a temporary tape. You'll have plenty of rehearsal time for the real thing."

"I know. But I hate it anyway. It upsets me."

"Right. Then you get grouchy."

"Yes, I do."

"And when you're grouchy, you become irrational."

"I don't become irrational!"

"You become irrational."

"I do not! I'm an actor, I'm emotional."

"And irrational."

"You don't understand actors."

"I *what*—? You're irrational right now."

He laughed. "You're right, I'm irrational. C'mon, let's get this thing done."

Stars are so used to having people pamper and agree with them on a shoot that acquiescence becomes its own nemesis. The more one agrees with a star, the more demanding and incorrigible he becomes. With Nolte, strong but friendly resistance is the only way to break through some of his fits. It disturbs the hell out of him, but he recognizes its strength and eventually surrenders to sanity.

And what's more, beneath his resentment, he actually enjoys the opposition. It's another game he can play: a matching of personality and wits.

"You know what my relationship is with you?" I asked him once.

"What?"

"I offer you ideas and insights so that you can be negative and contrary in order to work your way around to what I said in the first place."

"I'm not negative and contrary."

"There you go."

"Don't *do* that! And don't talk to me about me; talk to me about Jefferson. What is this? I don't see scene 104 in the schedule. Have they dropped scene 104?"

"I don't know. Maybe."

"I bet they've dropped it."

"I hope they haven't. It's a pivotal scene, Nick."

"No, it's not a pivotal scene. We can get along without it."

"I know we can. That's why I said pivotal and not critical."

"We don't need it. We see Maria with Lafayette. The audience will assume that she's separated from Jefferson. We don't have to have the tennis court scene (104). The audience will get it."

"Right. It's not critical."

"Well Jesus, Jim and Ismail probably saw it just the way I explained it, and they realized it wasn't necessary!"

"And they figured they could save a lot of money by dropping it."

"Well that too. But we really don't need it."

"True, it's not critical. It's pivotal though, because it sets up Jefferson's line about being separated from her by the crowds."

"Now there you go again. You always have to be right."

"I don't have to be, my friend. I just am."

"You're like Napoleon and Hitler. All you little guys have to always be right."

"Why, because I said it was pivotal?"

"It's not pivotal!"

"Change Jefferson's line about crowds separating them and then it's not even pivotal."

"I'm not going to change the line! It works just the way it is! Jesus—!"

He studied the script: scene 104 and Jefferson's line about the crowds. Then he mumbled softly, "But it sure would be nice to have this scene."

I smiled. "It certainly would."

He made a comical face. "It certainly would—it certainly would!"

"It would."

"But you don't have to say it that way: 'It certainly would.'"

I laughed. "I just said, 'It certainly would,' that's all."

"No, you didn't. You said, 'It certainly would' like 'I told you so.'"

"Well, you reversed yourself."

"No, I didn't. It's just that you always have to be right—you're always right."

"It's not that I'm always right; it's that you're always wrong."

He growled and gnashed his teeth. "I don't know why you're this way!"

"Because I've learned so much more than you."

"No, no, no—it's because you have to be superior."

"I don't have to be."

"Yes, you do."

"No, I don't have to be. I just am." I grinned at him.

He growled again and thrashed around. "Don't *say* that!"

"I never run away from the truth. You do. But I still love you. Despite it all, I still love—"

"*Despite it all—despite it all.* Y'see? That's not love, that's being judgmental."

"Certainly. All love is judgmental. Love has forgiveness in it, and if you're forgiving something, there had to be judgment there in the first place—"

"I don't want to hear it! I don't want to hear it!"

"So, you see? Despite your insanity, I still love you. C'mere an' lemme hug ya."

"Don't touch me! Don't touch me!" And he ran away, laughing.

"*It's a pivotal scene!*" I shouted.

The next day, he was gleefully recounting this exchange to Pauline when I walked into the makeup room.

"There he is, the man who'll never admit he's wrong."

Grinning, we played the game out for Pauline and Betty.

"There's no need to. I never am."

"You're arrogant."

"When one is right and good, he shouldn't be afraid to admit it."

"Well, you were wrong yesterday, and you upset me."

"*You* were wrong, and I think I'll put you on my shit list."

"I'm on *your*—?! You're on *mine!*" He turned toward Pauline. "He'll never apologize." Then back to me. "I'm willing to say I had a little fit if you'll admit you had one too."

"I'll tell you what—I'm willing to say you had a *major* fit and, despite everything, I still love you."

"There you go again—*despite everything*. That sounds like there's something wrong with me."

"There is."

"Jesus, you sound like my mother."

"Always listen to Mother. She knows what she's talking about. You want to run some lines?"

"Yeah, let's go."

We had to go through five minutes of laughter before we could get to the lines of the scene. But the exchanges had relaxed him. Nolte hasn't consciously recognized this about himself yet, but he needs someone near him to play his personality game, someone who will match him line for line, always with humor and never with contempt. When he can play that game, he becomes Nick again and not the tormented artist that acting forces him to be.

Apparently, he has that kind of relationship in Malibu now with Alan Arkin. He admires Arkin greatly and recounts many of the things that Alan says to him, especially when the statements treat Nolte with fond and friendly disrespect.

"I called Alan the other day," he told me. "I said, 'Hello, Alan, it's me, Nick. I'm sorry to disturb you, but—' and he said, 'Well, if you're sorry to disturb me, you shouldn't be calling.' And he hung up on me. He's great."

Ten

Nick Nolte never looks at dailies or video playbacks or, in most cases, even his own completed films. He believes watching dailies is counter-productive. He knows that everyone who watches the previous day's work views it only from the standpoint of his own personal interest. Sound men listen to sound. Makeup artists study make-up. Directors of photography see lighting and camera work. Actors cringe in the errors of their delivery. And everyone feels he could or should have done it better.

"It can't help me to watch dailies," he maintains. "If I don't like what I see, it can only make me feel lousy because I know we're not going to go back and shoot it again. And if I feel lousy, I'll be all screwed up for the next day's work."

However, Nick always feels the need to know what his work looks like to someone else. Knowing that everyone is watching dailies with no special interest in *his* acting, Nolte turns to his assistant for an honest reaction. Well, not entirely honest, because a negative word from his assistant will throw him into a depression as deep as any he could experience by viewing the dailies himself.

Eric accepted this responsibility of watching dailies and

then reporting to Nick with the same kind of conscientiousness that characterized the fulfillment of all his other duties. And because he understands that Nolte can accept only positive statements, Eric eliminates the negative.

"No sense telling him the whole truth," he will say. "The ship has left the dock."

Of course, he's right. With Nick, nothing good can come from the whole truth. Once, I made the mistake of suggesting that something could have been done a little better. The next morning, he accused me of keeping him awake all night. Poking produces pain; stroking quiets nerves. The ship has left the dock, so look to the horizon.

There were over 250,000 feet of film shot by the end of the schedule. Eric watched almost every foot of it. And since I was helping Nolte, I watched, too.

"How'd it go?" Nick would ask immediately upon our return from screening the previous day's footage. He could never go to sleep without hearing the report. And his questions always searched for comforting affirmation.

The last major scene that Nick had to film concerned the most dramatic moment in the screenplay. It drew the entire Jefferson-Sally Hemings-Patsy triangle into a shattering confrontation. It would take place in Jefferson's study at his *de Langeac* home. However, space in the room was so limited only key personnel were admitted. Cramped quarters, street and airplane noise problems and an appreciation of the scene's importance seemed to goad everyone into a state of nervousness and anxiety.

Nick's nerves were as taut as violin strings. "I don't know what I'm doing anymore. I've lost all track of continuity. I'm just going scene-by-scene."

"Well you know this scene so you're safe."

"I'm not safe."

"You've been working your ass off for almost a year. Are you telling me you don't understand what you've been working on?"

"No, I'm not saying that."

"Then cool it. It's just another scene and one that you understand thoroughly. Trust yourself, for Chrissake, trust yourself."

But under the circumstances, he couldn't, and his apprehensions escalated into outright paranoia.

The scene was numbered 138. In it, Sally Hemings and her brother James confront Jefferson with their intention to escape slavery by remaining in Paris. Sally is now pregnant with Jefferson's child; James's bitterness and anger are almost boundless. Jefferson finesses the situation and negotiates an agreement to have them return with him to Monticello. Patsy is called into the room to witness a Bible oath that he's compelled by James to swear.

Lengthy as well as important, scene 138 covered five and two-eighths pages. (In the real world, two-eighths becomes one-quarter, but never in filming; there eighths continue to be the page measurement.) The critical question to James Ivory and Pierre Lhomme became: How can we film such a long scene in such close quarters and keep it moving and interesting? In so tight a space, free use of tracks for the camera dolly was impossible. The only way to do it, they concluded, was to break the scene down into numerous close shots. Pierre Lhomme calculated it would take eighteen separate setups to get what was needed. There was no other way. If the full power of 138 were to be captured, everything had to be dissected into bits and pieces.

The first assistant director informed everyone, "This scene is going to be broken into so many shots, we'll have to shoot it out of *line* sequence. If you feel you have to run the scene to get into the actual line we'll be shooting, just ask."

For Nolte, the question became "If they're going to break everything down into bits and pieces, how the hell will I ever sustain the emotional juices of the scene when it's been fragmented that extensively?"

Ivory and Lhomme agreed that the success of 138 rested as much on the effectiveness of the camera as it did on the effectiveness of the acting. As a result, James Ivory relinquished most of his director's authority to his cinematographer.

Oddly, nothing had been transcribed as a check list. Here they were, going into a major, climactic scene that required special timing, pacing and intensity within every kind of shot the confining quarters would allow and nothing had been put on paper! It was all in Pierre Lhomme's head, all eighteen setups! Occasionally, Pierre forgot something he had created earlier; then he, Ivory, the camera operator and the 1st AD huddled to find the lost idea. After successfully completing a shot, Pierre and the camera operator would discuss the next setup, resolving problems in the harmony of their memories.

And while these discussions took place, Ivory left the room, turning the set over to them, the technicians and the stand-ins.

The crew sensed the special importance of 138. They became even more efficient than usual. Spots were marked as soon as stand-ins were set; the camera was moved into place immediately after a decision had been reached; lights were adjusted the moment a need was understood. There was no frenzy, though, just a pervasive mood of concentrated energy.

The tension was more than Nolte could bear. For the first time in the entire production, his distress revealed itself on the set. He became testy, difficult. Suggestions made by Pierre for special setups met with resistance. He withdrew into himself, not as an actor reaching for Thomas Jefferson, but as Nolte suffering disturbing thoughts. He became curt, blunt.

"You can't sit there," Nick said.

"Why not?"

"You'll be in my line of vision. I can't concentrate. You have to move. Get out."

And, finally, his anxiety overflowed into expressed dissatisfaction with what he felt was being done.

Both Jim and Pierre attempted to reassure him. Everything was going well. It was tedious, they knew, but they were getting what they wanted. His Jefferson was strong, very moving. The scene would look excellent in the dailies.

Nolte was not mollified. He'd convinced himself that more attention and concern were going into Pierre's lighting than into the importance of this moment to Thomas Jefferson.

The next night, he waited for the report on the dailies.

"Well, how were they?" he asked as soon as we entered his rooms.

"Outstanding!" I responded. "Blew me away!"

He seemed unimpressed, unmoved. "Yeah?"

"We saw all the *de Langeac* takes from yesterday," Eric said. "You were on-screen for a few of them, but the emphasis was on Sally and James."

"I know what I was in," he snapped sourly.

"We'll see your takes probably on Saturday," Eric offered.

"But what we saw is outstanding, so far," I added. "Powerful. Moving. The nuances were there. Everything worked. And even though you were off-screen, your voice and your interpretation were just right. When it's cut together, the scene's going to be memorable."

And Eric added, "It's great, Nick. Really. The lighting is soft and muted—"

"So, what else is new?" he said.

"We get the whole thing in this scene," I explained. "Everything you've worked on. The depth of the Jefferson-Sally relationship; the James-Sally, brother-sister love; the slavery issue; Patsy's suffering—everything."

He was unimpressed. "Well then, they have it. They don't need anything on me."

"Hey, you're going crazy again. As Eric said, we'll see your takes on Saturday—"

"Yeah. But they didn't do much on me. Pierre was so excited with Sally all he wanted to do was shoot her."

"And did he?"

"He would have, but Jim thought they had enough coverage on her."

"So what are you talking about?"

"Well, I just feel like I'm out of it."

"Out of what?"

"The whole scene. I feel like it's about Sally and James, and I'm there just to help them along."

"We haven't seen what they shot of you yet," Eric said. "And you have some more to finish up tomorrow—"

"I know," Nick cut him off, "but I don't feel like I'm *in* it! I mean, I go there and work my ass off all day so Thandie and Seth can look good."

"And they're there to help you when Jim shoots you," Eric answered.

"Yeah, I know, but by the time we do my takes, I'm all used up. I don't know what I'm doing. I don't know if it'll be good—"

"You couldn't screw it up now if you tried." I was becoming annoyed.

"Jesus, you don't understand!"

"No, *you* don't understand."

"By the time they did my takes, Seth and Thandie were used up. They had nothing more to give, so I had nothing to play off!"

"You mean, they weren't there for you? That's bullshit. They were there."

"Yes—they were there! But they didn't—aw, what the fuck—never mind, never mind, forget it! I don't want to talk about it anymore. Forget it!"

He turned away in anguish and frustration.

The next morning, Pierre approached Nick and, with his palms together in front of his face, Hindu fashion, he requested Nolte's cooperation in reshooting one of the previous day's takes. It was a gentle request, almost a plea, from a kind and sensitive man.

Nick seemed puzzled, but he agreed. His madness was still on him, though, and he found support for it in the request.

"I knew he was going too dark when he shot me yesterday," Nick argued later. "Sure, he was so caught up with Thandie and Seth, he didn't give a shit about me."

"Then why is he reshooting the angle of you near the window if he doesn't care about you?"

"Because I said something to James! I told him I was in the shadows and that the scene was becoming Thandie's and Seth's!"

"I don't think so," Eric joined in. "I think he's just trying to match the lighting."

"No, no, no! I'm telling you, Pierre fucked up and he probably realized it or maybe Jim said something to him, and now he's got to redo it!"

"We'll see," Eric said, trying to calm him. "They're having a special two o'clock screening for us. I spoke with Diane, the dailies editor. She asked Jim. He said it's okay."

"Good. I have to know. I think I know what happened, but I have to know."

"You're obsessing again, Nick."

"*Yes*, I'm obsessing! I give Pierre everything he asks for. I'm always there for him, and then he screws me by not caring about *me*! You know what that means? I can't trust him anymore! That's why he's shooting the scene over again, that's why he's got his hands up in front of his face that way—because he knows he fucked up, because he knows I'm pissed!"

"Look, you're concerned, we've made your concern known to Jim, he's willing to let us see the dailies even before *he* sees them, we'll see them this afternoon instead of Saturday, and then we'll know exactly what's happening. Until then, all of this is crazy speculation!"

"Then, you'll see them today?"

"We just said that, didn't we?"

"Good. I have to know."

At two o'clock, Eric and I sat in the screening room with Diane and watched the takes in question.

They were extraordinary! Strong, beautiful, everything they could and should have been. Nick was magnificent in them. He was Thomas Jefferson, not the legend, not the American icon, but the *man*, the human being, the deeply troubled father and lover, who was defending himself with incredible restraint in the throes of tremendous personal conflict. Pierre had covered him every way imaginable. The lighting and angles were artistic, effective, totally correct. And Jefferson's power didn't let down for a second. Tied to Thandie's, Seth's and Gwyneth's passions, the scene would bring chills to an audience and cap the film with meaningful and memorable force, provided James Ivory cut it effectively in the editing room. Everything Nolte had been eating himself raw about had, of course, been utterly ridiculous.

Returning to the Ritz Hotel, Eric and I were high from what we'd just seen. We evaluated. We laughed. We speculated. We concocted sadistic scenarios.

"You know what we ought to tell him?" Eric said.

"What?"

"We ought to tell him Humbert was there, and he hated everything!"

"Good. We'll tell him Humbert said, 'These are the first dailies I've seen that made me want to throw up!'"

"I'll tell him Humbert went home to sit in his kitchen and watch the wallpaper—he said it would be more exciting!"

Nick was waiting expectantly.

"Well?"

"Humbert was there. He said he's going home to sit in his kitchen and look at the wallpaper," I started.

Nolte seemed puzzled, slightly alarmed. "What?"

"He said it would be more interesting."

"Huh?"

"I'm only kidding. They were sensational, Nick. Really."

"They were, Nick," Eric agreed.

"You panicked over nothing. They're great."

"It wasn't over nothing," he persisted. "You haven't

seen the new scene. You really can't tell yet."

"Jesus Christ, we don't have to see the new scene! What they have works perfectly. The only problem Jim's going to have is making his choices in the editing room, there's so much outstanding stuff there!"

"No! You can't say that until you've seen *every*thing!"

Eric and I threw up our hands and left his suite.

Later, Nick tapped on my door. "Can I come in?"

"Come on in."

"You think I'm being an asshole over this."

"Hell, yes. Let it go already."

"It's just that I'll never be able to trust Pierre anymore."

"C'mon, will ya? Pierre's a cinematographer. Cinematographers are interested in their shots. You're part of the shot, so he's interested in you, too. He *has* to be. Especially if he's as good as Pierre is. You're making more of this thing than it ever deserved. It's time to drop it."

A long, thoughtful silence followed. Finally, Nick nodded his head. "Maybe you're right," he conceded.

"I'm always right. I thought you knew that by now." A wide grin accompanied my statement.

His grin was wider. "Fuck you!"

"Fuck you, too, my friend! Now get some sleep."

It had ended. The madness had finally worn itself out.

The next day, Eric and I watched all the takes again with Jim and Pierre. The re-shot scene was good, too, but it added nothing to the rest of the excellent footage. There had been no urgent need to re-shoot it other than Pierre Lhomme's penchant for perfection. When the rushes ended and the lights went on, we congratulated Jim and Pierre and told them how wonderful we felt the dailies were.

Both were pleased. Both smiled. Both said, "Thank you."

But Ivory added with some urgency, "I hope you'll tell that to Nick."

And Pierre nodded his head. "Tell Nick, will you? Please. Tell Nick."

Obviously, besides torturing himself, Nolte's paranoia had given these gentle men hours of unnecessary concern. And to their credit, the ugly incident was quickly forgiven and even more quickly forgotten.

It came to an end. Finally. After ten months of unrelenting study and preparation, which had included thirteen long weeks of intensive acting, Nolte heard the magical words he'd only been dreaming about.

"Okay, that does it. Thank you, everybody, that's a wrap!"

Indeed, there was magic in the announcement. Because as soon as it was made, Nick Nolte was transformed. In what seemed like an instant, his surliness disappeared. His entire demeanor changed. He grinned and laughed. He mingled with everyone. He even seemed to stand straighter. Now, he was ready to live again. He even talked freely of his plans. He was going back to California. He was taking a four-month vacation. He was going to live with Vicki and really give his love for her a chance. And he was going to spend a lot of time with his son Brawley.

He was Nick again, not the tormented artist who had doubted his own impressive talents, not the demented actor who had withdrawn from most of the *Jefferson in Paris* social experience in order to conserve his limited energies. He was Nick. Expansive. Communicative. Energetic. And ready to party.

In the few times he'd socialized during the shoot, Nolte would look longingly at the drink in everyone's hand. But he *never* ordered an alcoholic beverage for himself. Not even a beer. He'd clown and ask if he could sniff the bottles, and he'd hold them lovingly and whimper comically every time someone would order another drink. But being an admitted alcoholic, he understood clearly what a lapse in his fortitude could mean to his Jefferson characterization and, therefore, to the entire production.

Now, though, he was ready to slip. It was as if an enormous weight had been lifted from him. All commitments had been honored. All responsibilities had been met. He was free and flying. So what if a few drinks would throw him into a wild tailspin? So what if a crazy binge would fill him later with self-hatred and remorse? That would be something to worry about tomorrow. For today, it was—PARTY TIME!

The huge, Ismail Merchant wrap party was to take place the next evening. But that was a full day away. What about tonight? Wasn't there anything that could be done that night?

Of course, there was. We were in Paris; there were countless places waiting to be explored! That night, Nolte's two-day binge began.

He started early. He began his drinking at the usual, end-of-week get-together, which happened to be the wrap party that he'd finally been convinced to sponsor. The booze flowed. And Nick made sure he had his share. By the time people began to disperse, he was feeling a glorious glow.

About six of us decided, then, to continue the evening. Someone suggested a nightclub. Great idea! Laughing and sometimes even screaming enthusiastically, we piled into cars and took off for a nearby café. More drinking there. Then it was time to try another place. A small nightclub. The place was mobbed, but Nick's presence always guaranteed a table anywhere. We used him, and he was in a condition by now that no use of his celebrity could bother him. About an hour of drinking there made everyone ready for the next place. *The Bain-Douche!*

The *Bain-Douche* was a former bathhouse that had been converted to a disco nightclub. An *in* place of Paris at that time. Crowds of hopefuls blocked the entrance, pleading and arguing to get in. And powerful-looking guards pushed and shoved them away from the doors.

Again, Nolte's celebrity became our "Open Sesame!"

Inside, the place was a madhouse, so crowded it was almost impossible to move, with some of the most beautiful women one could find anywhere, jerking and gyrating rapturously on a tiny dance floor to music so loud it was necessary for non-dancers to put mouth to ear in order to be heard.

Nolte wasn't interested in the women, although it was very clear that some of them could become very interested in him. He found the bar. More drinking.

By now, all of us were feeling gloriously numb. Even Stanislas, our gentle and controlled driver, whose screaming mispronunciation of "MOTHERFUCKER!!!!" never failed to reduce Nolte and everyone else to helpless heaps of laughter.

By 5:00 A.M., after more booze and rambling and singing our way through Paris streets, and after standing

on a curb and peeing endlessly into the gutter like a cho-
rus line of gargantuan bladders, everyone agreed it was
time to go home, get some sleep and prepare ourselves for
the BIG wrap party that night. Everyone, that is, except
Nolte. For Nick, there were still some hours left to be
enjoyed. No amount of persuasion could change his
mind. And what's more, he insisted on being left to his
own devices. What he planned, he wouldn't say. Where
he intended to go, he wouldn't say. What he demanded,
though, was the freedom to be alone. There was no arguing with him. So he was left on his own.

To this day, no one knows where he went or what he
did. And that's probably true for Nolte, too. But he
returned to the Ritz Hotel at nine-thirty that morning
and instead of going to sleep, he stayed up all day drinking.

Partying stretched into Ismail's final celebration. A
magnificent affair. Over two hundred people came from
all over Paris to join the festivities. Food everywhere. A
river of champagne. Big band music. Dancing. Laughter.
An endless, escalating spirit of camaraderie and joy. Even
quiet, reserved James Ivory took to the dance floor for a
wild rumba with Greta Scacchi.

Nick just drank.

But not alone. One of the young production assistants attached herself to him, and they were never seen
without each other. The hours passed. Whenever we
looked for Nolte, we found him with the girl, heads
together in intimate conversation, her smile languorous,
his expression drunkenly intense. Around two o'clock, we
felt it was necessary to separate them.

Nick and I were scheduled to leave on the Concorde
for the States at 11:00 A.M. Eric wouldn't be going back

with us. He was moving on to Spain for a rendezvous with a lovely girl to whom he'd been introduced by Gwyneth Paltrow.

Everyone was becoming concerned about Nolte. Especially James Ivory and Ismail Merchant, who saw in Nick's worsening condition something unpredictable and self-damaging.

"Don't you think he'd be better off if you took him back to the Ritz now?" Ivory asked worriedly.

"I'm trying, Jim, but he won't leave. Talk to him. See what you can do."

Ivory pleaded with Nick, without any more success than anyone else was having.

When Nolte goes on one of his tears, almost nothing can get through to him. He has to run it out. Fortunately, since becoming a member of Alcoholics Anonymous, that happens very infrequently now. But when it does, he becomes granite in his determination to do as he pleases.

"Isn't there something we can do?" Ismail asked anxiously.

"Maybe this'll work. I'll make him believe he's on his own, but you tell the girl he has to get back to the hotel, and that she should insist on getting him there because she has some work to do for you early in the morning."

To make my point, I said goodnight to Nolte and left with my date.

The plan must have worked. Slowly. Because I was in bed with my lady by 2:30, and she remarked at 4:30, "I think I heard Nick go into his room."

She was right.

Nolte is truly remarkable when it comes to meeting an obligation. Any obligation. He knew even in his drunken stupor that we had to check out of the Ritz by nine. He knew that we had to be awake by eight, at the latest, if we hoped to wash, dress and grab something to eat, assuming we'd be able to eat after all that drinking. And here he was coming in at 4:30, blind drunk, with no guarantee that he would ever wake up again once he'd fallen asleep. But he was obliged to make that flight.

I'll never know where he finds his stamina. But only three hours later, he was tapping on my door and whispering, "Hey, are you awake in there? C'mon, will ya? Get up. We've got a plane to catch."

And when I opened the door, he stood there seemingly sober, washed, fully dressed and frowning like a troubled schoolboy.

It was in the airport that he fell apart completely.

As he slouched in an armchair of the Concorde waiting room, guilt and remorse overtook him like a fatal disease. He was so sick at heart, he could barely talk.

"How could I have done that? Jesus, what's the matter with me? I was bad, wasn't I? I was disgustingly bad."

"You might say that."

"What did I do? I don't remember."

"Well, you had a lot of people worried."

"Oh, shit."

"Especially Jim and Ismail."

"Ohhhh, shit!"

"They'll get over it, though. Sooner than you will."

"But I didn't hurt anybody, did I?"

"We-e-ell."

"Oh, my god, don't tell me I hurt somebody! Please, I didn't hurt anybody, did I?"

"No. You just scared the hell out of the girl."

"What'd I say? What'd I do?"

"I don't know. You were just hanging all over her."

"Oh, god."

"She brought you home, didn't she?"

"Yeah."

"Good. We planned that. Did she stay with you?"

"Yeah."

"Did she go to bed with you?"

"Yeah. I think so. I don't know. Oh, man, what am I gonna do?"

His remorse had him on the verge of tears.

"Take it easy. We'll write her a note when we get home."

"Yeah… yeah….I have to apologize to her...I *must*."

"And Jim and Ismail."

"Yeah….oh, goddamn me...what's the *matter with me*?!"

"You danced with the devil, buddy, and he stomped all over you."

"I gotta get him out of me, though! As soon as we get home. I have to go into detox…."

"Betty Ford?"

"No. But I know a place. And I have to get back to AA right away."

"Good. AA's your grounding. It strengthens your conscience so you can resist the devil's call."

"Yeah. Oh, man, I'm suffering."

It was no momentary pang of regret. It was deep and lasting. It sprang from a bottomless well of conscience. He was concerned with himself, of course—his narcissism always dictates that—but this time he was truly more worried about others. He wasn't sure about it, but if he had slept with the girl, he'd been unfaithful to Vicki. And Vicki had never done anything to deserve that. Vicki deserved only the best he was able to offer.

Fidelity wasn't too much to expect of him.

And Merchant and Ivory deserved the same kind of respect they had shown him. They had never ignored his needs. They had always responded to his concerns. They deserved not to have their needs and their concerns ignored by him.

Nolte is very interesting that way: though he rarely extends himself to help others, he, nevertheless, recognizes a responsibility to them, and he tries to live within the parameters of that awareness. When he fails, and he believes they've been injured by his failure, guilt will gnaw at him like a voracious worm.

Eleven

It took Nick a few days to recover physically from his Paris binge. Just being with Vicki helped. They were together in New York for about a week before he went down to Florida to be with his son. He rested. He slept. He returned to a sensible eating regimen. It took many months, however, for his conscience to heal.

When we parted, I told him I expected to be in California for a few days soon.

"There are some people I have to see. Have the guest house ready."

"No, no, Jesus, no," he insisted quickly. "We gotta get away from each other for a while!"

It never occurred to him that we didn't have to see each other, that we could respect each other's privacy. Why? Because extended intimacy makes Nick Nolte very nervous. Something seems to wear out in the relationship, and he becomes uncomfortable then with the mere thought of physical proximity. That's when he needs time to recover. If only ten months of our closeness could produce this kind of response, I wondered how long he and

Vicki would be able to stay together.

"Hello, Nicko," I asked, "how're you feeling?"

"Better."

"Been drinking lately?"

"Not a drop. When're you coming out to LA?"

"Why do you ask?"

"We're having a screening of *Jefferson in Paris*."

"When?"

"In about four weeks."

Four weeks later, in the lobby of Creative Artists Agency, Nick was extremely anxious. He smiled and joked and seemed affable enough with the small crowd of Hollywood powermeisters that prepared to go into the screening room, but his nervousness showed when he whispered, "Where are you going to sit?"

"I don't know," I answered. "Maybe with Ismail."

"Sit with me."

"Why?"

"I don't want to be alone."

"You wouldn't be alone."

"Sit with me."

"Okay."

He chose two seats on the far right aisle. "I'll take the end one in case I have to get out of here fast."

Watching himself is usually pure torture for Nolte. Especially in the company of Hollywood fault-finders. When the lights went down and the picture started, he actually positioned himself facing the wall so that he was compelled to look at the screen almost furtively over his left shoulder. However, as the film progressed, his body turned slowly until he was sitting in a normal manner.

"It's good, Nick. You're Jefferson," I whispered.

"Some people won't think so, but they won't know what Jefferson was."

"Yeah," he whispered in return. "We got him."

He was pleased with his work. Pleased enough to say later, "It was comfortable. I even did something I never do: I relaxed enough to appreciate all the other things in the picture. Jim and Pierre did a fantastic job."

All traces of his Paris agonies had long-since disappeared. The entire experience had become something to be remembered fondly, something to be added happily to the collection of stories that would entrance future listeners on future shoots.

Only two developments took shape to mar his pleasure and his satisfaction. The first was the reaction of Joe Roth, chairman of the Walt Disney Studios, which had financed and was preparing to distribute *Jefferson in Paris*. And the second was the review by Roger Ebert, nationally known film critic.

"Joe told me he doesn't think it'll appeal to the nineteen-year-olds," Nick said.

"What does that mean?"

"Probably that they're not going to push it."

"No advertising?"

"Minimal."

"How many theaters?"

"As few as possible."

"Then it'll be in and out in two weeks."

"Probably, unless it gets rave reviews all around."

But *Jefferson in Paris* did not get "rave reviews all around." Actually, critical reactions were split. Some were hot with praise; some were tepid and uncertain; some were unequivocally cold and hostile. A few reviewers thought Nolte's Jefferson was extraordinary; others thought he was a deadly bore.

One reviewer who was not favorably impressed was Roger Ebert.

"Did you see Siskel and Ebert last night?" Nick asked me.

"Never watch them."

"Siskel thought it was terrific—a strong thumbs-up; Ebert found it disappointing—thumbs down. He said I was lackluster as Jefferson, that I didn't do justice to the complexity of the man, that I didn't have a sense of his emotional life, of who Jefferson was, and that I was too cold and distant."

"And what did Siskel say?"

"He said the movie is explosive. He said it's sumptuous and serious, literate and passionate. He said it deals with slavery issues and love and all the complexity of the man's life, and that it will be marvelously controversial."

"And what did he say about you?"

"He said I was great and a wonderful choice to play Jefferson."

"Well, that shows you: Siskel knows what he sees; Ebert sees only what he thinks he knows."

"Y'know what I'd like to do?"

"What?"

"I'd like to send Ebert a letter."

"Why?"

"Oh, I don't know. Just to open his eyes, I guess."

"What do you want to do, attack him?"

"Not really. But it'd be nice to jab him a little."

"What's this all about? You've never cared what reviewers say."

"I know. But this is different. How'd you like five hundred dollars?"

"You want me to write the letter, right?"

"Yeah. A long one."

"Educate the man?"

"Something like that."

"Do you have a copy of the review?"

"No."

"Have Sherri get one and fax it to me."

I received the fax a few days later.

The letter to Roger Ebert *was* long. Almost four pages, single spaced. And it was informative, too. It addressed Ebert's criticism point by point. It described fully what kind of man Jefferson had been, what Nolte had tried to do, and what the film was all about.

First, it explained Nick's early preparation: how he had investigated Jefferson's frame of mind when he left for France in 1784, what Jefferson had experienced in the years before his departure, and how deeply the calamities had affected him.

It depicted Jefferson as a broken man, condemned for his failures as the war-time governor of Virginia and utterly devastated by the deaths of his wife and daughter. It informed Ebert that Jefferson's crushed spirit wouldn't even allow him to attend the country's great victory celebration after Cornwallis's surrender to Washington, signaling the end of the war and American independence. That Jefferson was able to function at all as Ambassador to France was something of a miracle, the letter suggested. Lackluster? Certainly not. More accurately, a beaten man of incredible self-restraint—something Ebert, as a film critic, should have appreciated in the accuracy of Nick's performance.

The letter went on to enumerate Jefferson's many interests, and it chided the reviewer's failure to recognize them. Furthermore, it expressed surprise at his inability to see the political metaphor of the film—the conflict between the new concept of American Democracy and the outmoded governments of European Monarchy. It even explained the sexual affair between Thomas Jefferson and his teenage slave, Sally Hemings, within the context of this tyranny vs. freedom struggle, detailing the relationship in a way that could educate the film critic and steer him away from his superficial reactions. And lastly, it invited Ebert to see the film again and to evaluate Nick's performance in light of this explanation.

It was a good letter, if I say so myself, good enough for Nolte to call me as soon as he'd read it and to gush:

"It's great!"

"Says what you want him to know?"

"Perfect!"

"No changes?"

"No…nothing…I like it just the way it is."

"Now what?"

"Now I'll have Sherri type it up on my stationery, and I'll sign it."

"Think he'll respond?"

"I dunno."

"If he does, send me a copy of whatever you get from him."

"Okay…and thanks, Mel, thanks a lot."

"Hey, if you like it that much, send me another five hundred."

It certainly would have been interesting to hear or read Roger Ebert's reaction. But Roger never had an opportunity to react because Nolte never sent him the letter. He never explained fully why he had changed his mind. But in my understanding of the man, I'd guess that he saw the folly in playing this particular game. Nick understands very well that no matter what he could have said to Ebert, Roger was in a superior position because he would always have the final word. The game was a no-win match for Nick. And if there's one thing Nolte always tries to avoid, it's a contest that he suspects he doesn't stand a chance of winning.

There's no doubt that negative reviews helped to discourage Disney from investing extensively in the picture's advertising budget. But that may not have been the only reason for the studio's failure to support it.

Jefferson in Paris had been a Jeffrey Katzenberg project. By the time the picture was ready for theaters, the Katzenberg-Eisner battle had produced Jeffrey's resignation and departure from the company with the threat of a major lawsuit hanging over Disney's corporate head. Joe Roth could not have been expected to put himself and Michael Eisner in an embarrassing position. It would be better to let the picture die quickly and to swallow the $13,000,000 loss than to help it to some success, which would only have made Jeffrey Katzenberg's production judgments look good.

It's quite possible that Nolte's career was caught in the company's bitter wrangling. Whatever the reason, the film's box-office failure weighed heavily on him. His last truly successful picture had been *Prince of Tides*. It had catapulted him into an Academy Award nomination, with everyone believing he was the favorite to win the Oscar for Best Actor. He was a studio Golden Boy, even on the cover of *People* magazine as "The Sexiest Man Alive!"

In truth, none of that means anything to Nolte. He was interested in it only to the extent that it would bring him even better acting opportunities. It did. Manuscripts poured into his office at an even greater rate than before; producers called constantly with all kinds of offers. But Nick has a predilection for choosing difficult, noncommercial vehicles. So, between *Prince of Tides* and *Jefferson in Paris*, his choices put him into four films that were clearly not box office successes: *Lorenzo's Oil*, *I'll Do Anything*, *Blue Chips* and *I Love Trouble*.

Hollywood baseball is something like Major League baseball: three strikes and you're out! You may go down swinging magnificently, your work may be greatly admired even in the films' failures, but the fact of the matter is you've struck out!

Nolte was hoping that *Jefferson in Paris* would end his slump. It didn't. After the picture's release, he went into *Mulholland Falls*, *Mother Night*, and *U-Turn*, all of which display his acting talent superbly and clearly—none of which touched general audiences positively.

Following *Mother Night*, in which he plays a World War II double agent who commits suicide after posing as a hateful Nazi propagandist, Nick wondered about his acting career.

"I think I'm winding down," he told me.

"Why do you say that?"

"Studio interest isn't what it used to be."

"It's all box office."

"I know. I may have to retire soon."

"It could all turn around tomorrow. One big success. That's all it takes in Hollywood."

"But that would mean I have to go for the commercial stuff. And I can't do that. I tried it with *I Love*

Trouble, and besides being a box office failure, the picture didn't give me any satisfaction at all."

"You don't have to go studio commercial. You can still pick your troubled, off-beat characters, but there's no reason why they have to be so damned unappealing. It's possible to play someone an audience can feel for and hope for, y'know."

"But it's got to be meaningful."

"Who says troubled people can't be decent and meaningful?"

"Yeah, I guess so. Well, we'll see. Meanwhile, I think I'll take some advice I got recently. I was talking with Sean Penn. He's got the right idea. I'm gonna stay with the independent producers. They're trying to do different things. And that's what I like."

And that's exactly what he's done.

His two most recent releases, Paul Schrader's *Affliction* and Terrence Malick's *The Thin Red Line*, are proof of his determination, and both reveal the stunning magnitude of his talent. So outstanding is his work in *Affliction* that it was hailed in *The New York Times* as "...the performance of his career," and by *The Wall Street Journal* as "...a great performance by a great actor at the top of his form." As of this writing, it has earned him a Golden Globe Best Actor nomination and the New York Film Critics Circle Best Actor award. And if it doesn't get him an Oscar, as *The Wall Street Journal* says: "...there's no justice under the sun or among the stars."

In a telephone conversation only minutes before typing these words (yes, we're still quite close despite his opposition to this book and his refusal to read it), he spoke with the ebullience of a man who has been snatched from the lip of an abyss.

Once again, his career is ascendant. Once again, he's excited about the entire process of making motion pictures. It's as if a wonderful new chapter, filled with promise and hope, is being written in his life. Indeed, it has all turned around for him.

"...one big success—that's all it takes in Hollywood."

Offers will flood his way now. The studios will be on him with money and what they believe to be "meaningful" projects. But knowing Nick as I do, I'm confident he'll continue to go his own way.

He's paid for this right in alcoholism, friendless insulation and failed marriages. He's dedicated himself to the pursuit of his freedom, to living a life unimpeded by external authority, one in which he makes all the decisions without being frustrated by troublesome opposition. But what's unfortunate is that, although this hunger for individuality *has* produced long strides of accomplishment, these steps have been disturbingly solitary. With Nolte, it's always "follow me or be left behind."

As a result, people *are* left behind. People who care deeply for him. People who want only the best for him. Always following anybody can become tiresome and discouraging. Inevitably, those closest and dearest to Nick separate themselves from him, and he's left alone to ponder the vicissitudes of his life and to criticize others for their inability to sustain the bonds of unconditional love.

Eric is moving out on his own now. It's time for him to be more in the industry than an assistant to Nick Nolte. After almost a dozen pictures with him, it's time for Eric to try his hand at producing.

And Vicki made a decision about Nick, too. She moved off the estate and into her own apartment. She felt that her life with Nick wasn't as fulfilling as she had hoped it would be. She believed she'd lost something of herself in the relationship, and the only way to feel good about herself again was to be away from him. Not to be trailing after him, trying always to catch up. But something happened. After several months apart, she and Nick resolved their differences. Vicki gave up her apartment and returned to the estate. Clearly, her love for him runs very deep, and that's completely understandable.

Because once you've come to know Nick Nolte, once you've enjoyed his humor, his idiosyncrasies, his dedication, his passionate soul, once you've seen his heart, his concern, once you've shared his intellect, his obsessive demons and, yes, even his unbridled paranoia, no matter what pain he may have caused you, you will still, and always, care for him.

I know I do.

Epilogue

"Why do you call Nick an artist?" a friend asked me recently. "Don't you trivialize the word by applying it to an actor?"

"Not at all," I replied. "The instrument of self-expression doesn't really matter. It could be music, dance, painting, woodcarving, whatever. If art is the pursuit of some kind of truth, then the one who's actively pursuing it is the artist. But whether he's good, bad or indifferent is another matter. That's determined by the degree of his commitment and by his success in leading us to a truthful experience. As an actor, Nolte's commitment is total and, regardless of box office success or failure, no one doubts the truth of his work. His life may be a mass of aberrations, he may have great difficulty with relationships, he may be hounded by personal demons, but his search is always honest, and his acting is always pure."

Now, that discussion led me to consider Nick in relation to others on his level of achievement, and it became clear that, distinctive as he may appear to be, Nolte is not unique. Actually, he's representative of a particular level of artistry, a level that produces extraordinary results and, at the same time, inescapable corrupting influences.

Artists like Nolte are brilliant in their respective art forms but often tormented in their life pursuits. In their never-ending struggle for further liberation of their spirit, they suffer even as they create; but it's in the heat of that suffering that they are most alive. When opportunities to create no longer exist, the spirit shrivels and even dies. And the dread of that inevitable day hangs like a specter over their heads. However, the public doesn't often see this agony; it becomes known, usually, when it erupts in tabloid ugliness. Schizophrenia? Paranoia? Perhaps. Then how do they survive? Well, in the insulation of their celebrity, they form a quasi-secure community, one with its own morality, its own code of behavior, one in which, unfortunately and paradoxically, they rarely feel safe, complete and totally happy.

"Being true to yourself ain't easy," my friend stated.

Indeed.

However, Nick Nolte has been trying to do just that all his life. And, in respect to his acting, he has succeeded admirably.